MW00399771

This is a must read for anyone who wants to get a first-hand look at how God works through creating experiences in life that draw us closer to Him. Through his stories, Michael unpacks the power of the "SpringHill experience," bringing the message of Christ to kids in a meaningful and impactful way.

Bill Payne Former SpringHill Board Chair
Vice Chairman, Amway Corporation

Experience = Everything: Life Transformation the SpringHill Way is a glimpse into how Christ builds His Kingdom on earth through the hearts and the hands of His people. I have personally experienced SpringHill in a variety of capacities over many years: as a family camper and father of two children, and as a global ministry leader seeking holiness for myself and our staff. It is with the highest regard for my friend Michael Perry that I welcome this book and encourage you to explore for yourself what makes SpringHill so incredibly special.

John Heerema Executive Director, Biglife

It's been a wonderful privilege for us to have a front-row seat and witness the amazing ways God has used Springhill to impact the lives of not only kids, but of parents, grandparents, staff, volunteers, and supporters as well. Under Michael Perry's superb leadership, SpringHill has evolved from a beacon of Christ's love in Evart Michigan to a broader movement now reaching thousands of kids throughout the Midwest and beyond. This book is the inspiring story of God's love and faithfulness.

Dan Gordon Chairman of the Board, Gordon Food Services
Magee Gordon Former SpringHill Board Member

experience
=
everything

LIFE TRANSFORMATION
THE SPRINGHILL WAY

experience
=
everything

MICHAEL PERRY

WITH FOREWORD BY STEVE ANDREWS

Published by Advantage, Charleston, South Carolina.
Member of Advantage Media Group.

ADVANTAGE is a registered trademark, and the Advantage colophon is a trademark of Advantage Media Group, Inc.

Printed in the United States of America.

10 9 8 7 6 5 4 3 2 1

ISBN: 978-1-59932-924-6
LCCN: 2018945239

Book design by Carly Blake.

This publication is designed to provide accurate and authoritative information in regard to the subject matter covered. It is sold with the understanding that the publisher is not engaged in rendering legal, accounting, or other professional services. If legal advice or other expert assistance is required, the services of a competent professional person should be sought.

Advantage Media Group is proud to be a part of the Tree Neutral® program. Tree Neutral offsets the number of trees consumed in the production and printing of this book by taking proactive steps such as planting trees in direct proportion to the number of trees used to print books. To learn more about Tree Neutral, please visit **www.treeneutral.com.**

Advantage Media Group is a publisher of business, self-improvement, and professional development books and online learning. We help entrepreneurs, business leaders, and professionals share their Stories, Passion, and Knowledge to help others Learn & Grow. Do you have a manuscript or book idea that you would like us to consider for publishing? Please visit **advantagefamily.com** or call **1.866.775.1696.**

For my best friend and wife, Denise, who has always encouraged, believed in, and loved me. May our summers always be full of kids, faith, and fun. Also to our children, Jonathan, Mitch, Christina, MD, and his wife Carissa, who have always made our summers (and every other season of our life) full of the greatest joy.

TABLE OF CONTENTS

FOREWORD

Paula and I were never supposed to have kids. We were told by two infertility specialists that it just wasn't possible for us to have biological children. This was back at a time when adoption was pretty hard and expensive, so we were very discouraged.

But, by the grace of God, we ended up having a baby after four or five years of infertility. And when Lyndee was in fourth grade, she came home from church one day with a little flyer that said the fourth and fifth graders would be going to SpringHill for a retreat. Lyndee was really timid, not much of a risk taker. Yet she kept saying, "I really wanna go."

So she went on this retreat, and lo and behold, Lyndee came around to Christ that weekend at SpringHill.

It was so unbelievable because SpringHill was something I'd loved for years and, all of a sudden, our first daughter, the one we weren't supposed to have, made a public decision to follow Jesus ... as fourth grader!

Well, over the next seven or eight years, all four of our kids did the retreat, and it was incredibly formative for them. They all ended up being summer counselors there and learned so much about leadership and how to lead others to Christ. Some of our kids even went on to become area directors.

The SpringHill experience is a different kind of experience. It's coming to know Jesus, what it means to follow Jesus, and that following Jesus can be fun, but also challenging. It means making hard decisions and it means pushing yourself. Now my only granddaughter, Marguerite, is going to SpringHill's day camp this summer and is ready to have her first SpringHill experience with Jesus. It makes me weep with joy just thinking about it.

My forty-year journey with SpringHill began when I was hired as a junior high youth director at Ward Presbyterian Church back in the fall of 1978. We took about seventy-five junior high kids to SpringHill for the first retreat I ever led for Ward Church. We stayed in the cabooses, which was a really big deal back then. It was my first experience and it was a lot of fun. I met the founder, Enoch, and through the years I bumped into his son, Mark, from time to time. Enoch was such a dynamic leader and speaker, really the heart of what SpringHill is all about.

I remember when the mantle fell to Michael Perry to lead SpringHill. Michael had only come on in recent years, and I think that Michael's part in the SpringHill story, in many ways, is the best part. He's so charming and humble, and he's such a smart and self-effacing guy. The board at the time knew I was a huge cheerleader for SpringHill, and they were looking for a couple of church leaders to be on the board during the transition. Actually, it's the only board I've ever served on in my life.

Michael was trying to consolidate the movement of SpringHill in very uncertain times, and he hit the ground running and brought super-solid, non-flashy stability to SpringHill. Under his leadership, SpringHill exploded to 10,000 or more summer campers.

He started making great decisions and was really pouring into the board as well as into his staff and team. This guy took over SpringHill in a storm where God was moving things around and where we were riding a big ship through big water and across big waves. Michael just took that wheel and steadied the ship … and SpringHill didn't miss a beat.

Michael intuitively spotted the first big changes and trends in how families were operating and how dual income families were working. Michael really led the way for the board and realized we had to respond to the changes; if SpringHill stayed the same, it was going to die. Michael had the guts to recognize that. He kept pushing the board to reinvent SpringHill, and now, twenty years later, SpringHill has become a powerful voice in Christian camping all over America. What an incredible privilege it has been for me to be on that journey.

There's a saying I see embodied in Michael: "There's no limit to what you can accomplish if you don't care who gets the credit." That would be one of the bylines I would use for Michael Perry. He couldn't care less. He simply wants the kingdom of God to move forward. That's why he's led with humility and integrity as well as anybody I know.

In 1990, my partners and I launched Kensington Church. Our dream was to reach unchurched people who didn't know Christ and surprise them with a church experience that was fun, meaningful, appointed to where they live, and where their kids were beloved. They would be inspired to know Jesus Christ without guilt and shame, but with the hope that Jesus Christ brings. We did that, and miraculously it took off.

Through the years, God gave us one organizational kindred spirit, and that's SpringHill. Kensington people would go to SpringHill. They would feel like it was an extension of everything they had experienced at Kensington, and people from SpringHill would come and be a part of Kensington. SpringHill did such a great job of training young leaders who have come back to serve Kensington. I'll bet you half our staff at Kensington has worked at SpringHill at some point. SpringHill is a leadership factory.

I have an eight-piece, ministry-like mission for the twelve Kensington Campuses. One mission is a strategy of 110 U.S. church plants that we want to reach a couple hundred thousand people, and we're launching our 61st church later this fall. Another is our vision of having twenty indigenous church planting global partners who could help us come into different parts of the world and serve under indigenous leaders of those countries. We have eleven of those with my good friend Julius Murgor in Kenya. We've got six other objectives on that list, but number seven is that we help SpringHill achieve its goal of reaching hundreds of thousands of campers annually. SpringHill is actually one of Kensington's big, hairy, audacious goals. It's the only organization outside of our global partners that is part of the Kensington Forever Mission. That alone tells you how close we feel to SpringHill.

Hundreds of thousands of kids and adults have been touched through the SpringHill experience. I don't think you could find another Christian ministry in Michigan that has directly affected more lives through Jesus Christ than SpringHill. I don't think it's possible that there's any group that has brought the winsomeness, the beauty, and the hope of Jesus to the world like SpringHill.

At some point, Michael Perry won't be leading SpringHill. I won't be leading Kensington. But hopefully we'll be still serving the goals that God's called us to. Hopefully our teams of people will remain true to the vision that God has put in our hearts to see people come to Christ. Honestly, if anybody's done that better in this country than SpringHill, I'd like to see it. SpringHill's ability to reach multitudes of people for Christ is the best kept secret in America, and I've been blessed to be a part of it.

Steve Andrews

Co-founder/Lead Pastor

Kensington Church

Let the Journey Begin

ave you ever read a book that changed the way you experience life and faith? If not, you are in for a unique and life-transforming read. This is a different kind of book because SpringHill is a different kind of place. It's actually much more than a place, as you'll soon see. SpringHill is, above all else, an experience. And as the title suggests, experience is *everything*, especially where young people are concerned.

This book is in many ways like SpringHill: a blend of faith and fun, entertaining and informative and yet, tucked within every page are life lessons about God's love for us. You'll find each chapter begins with a callout, a lamp to light the way on your journey, to give guidance and context to each chapter. And at the end, you'll find a reflection section to give you a quiet moment to contemplate the themes and lessons provided in each chapter and to challenge you to better connect yourself to the stories, and to God.

Throughout your journey you'll also notice that the trail is marked with quotes and other callouts to help guide your experience and enhance your enlightenment and to demonstrate that this book is more than a collection of stories or a celebration of SpringHill's successes. It's more than a sum of fifty years of knowledge and experience and divine guidance and grace. This book is a map for you to follow. Not just any ordinary map, however, but a treasure map for discovering a life transformation, a map to create life-transforming moments for others in your life, and for living your life with the purpose and passion God intended so you may join Him in His exalted glory one day.

If you're a parent, grandparent, a youth, children's pastor leader, a teacher, or just someone who loves young people, we want to give you a glimpse into how SpringHill creates these life-changing experiences, and how you too can do the same. The goal of the book is to inspire, encourage, and equip those who love young people and want to see their lives transformed.

In my twenty years of working at SpringHill, I've seen time and again that something amazing happens to our campers, our staff, our summer leaders, our community partners, and our supporters when they open their hearts and minds to our experience. And we invite you to experience it now, for yourself.

Let the journey begin, The SpringHill Way.

ACKNOWLEDGEMENTS

Max DePree once said, "The first responsibility of a leader is to define reality. The last is to say thank you." As the senior leader at SpringHill, the Experience = Everything project reflects a fulfillment of this first responsibility. These Acknowledgments are my attempt to fulfill the last.

I'm grateful for Abby Netti and Mike Smith for their encouragement from day one of this project. Abby, in particular, has walked through each step, editing, providing feedback and comments and needed support. I'm also thankful for the staff at SpringHill, and in particular my leadership team, for being so good that I had space to devote time to creating *Experience = Everything*. It's a privilege to serve with such a talented team of people.

Thanks to the SpringHill Board of Directors, both past and present, for their encouragement and direction. They are remarkable, and are models of what not-for-profit boards should look like and do.

I'm grateful for the team at Advantage, who have shepherded me through this process with much grace and wisdom. In particular, I'm thankful for Chip St. Clair, who took my stories, thoughts, and words, made sense of them, and put it all together in an engaging and readable format.

As always, I continue to be indebted to my wife, Denise, who bears with my non-stop working, thinking, and dreaming. She did this once again during this project while providing invaluable input for *Experience = Everything*.

Finally, I'm eternally grateful to Jesus Christ for the purpose He's given to my life. Without Him, I'd be on a journey with no guide, compass, mission, or destination. He is truly my all in all. May this book be a small part of bringing His Kingdom values here to earth and thus glory to His Name.

The Red Truck

"I believe in Christianity as I believe that the sun has risen: not only because I see it, but because by it I see everything else."
—C. S. Lewis

Hope. Such a small word. Just one syllable. Only four letters. Yet that single, simple word has embodied and defined SpringHill from the very beginning, and it continues to describe SpringHill today, nearly fifty years and over half a million changed lives later.

It all started with a beat-up, 1952 Studebaker, and a man who wouldn't take no for an answer. Enoch Olson likely learned that lesson in persistence from the young Reverend Balmer, who made not one, not two, but *seven* attempts to persuade Enoch to take the reins as the camp's first director that summer of 1968. Yet Enoch's hesitant acceptance proved to be God's planning. The newly hired innovative director envisioned SpringHill as not just a different kind of camp but a different kind of ministry that integrated faith with fun, through teachable moments and unique activities, a vision that would foster a community in Christ.

A lot of miracles came together for Enoch in those early years. SpringHill only had one donated truck, that old Studebaker, and desperately needed something bigger and better to haul all the materials and equipment to build the first camp. What's worse is the new ministry had a shoestring budget already stretched to the point of nearly snapping.

Lo and behold! That Studebaker broke down one day on the way to pick up donations for the camp. Enoch prayed and, literally, walked to a nearby prominent construction company that just happened to have a fleet of new trucks. He sat down with the owner, Harold Shaw, and pleaded his case, explaining the need for a truck, and the lack of funds to pay for it. Harold turned him down flat. Enoch didn't balk but, instead, dove right back in and enthusiastically told the owner all about his vision for a new kind of Christian camp unlike anything anywhere else in the world. Not a chance.

Enoch demonstrated to Harold how he had no money at all, pulling out his pockets and going so far as to say he didn't even have money for dinner that night. For a half-hour, Enoch begged and pleaded and persisted, explaining how he had been praying night after night for a new truck for SpringHill.

But the owner wouldn't budge. No guilt trips, no sympathy, no compassion. Enoch sat stumped, unsure of what to do.

Exasperated, he held the eyes of the dealer. "Harold, have you ever seen a miracle?"

Harold shook his head. "There's no way I'm giving you a truck."

And then the construction company's accountant walked in, apparently attracted by the commotion. He asked Enoch about the camp and whether it was a registered nonprofit. Enoch, of course, replied that it was.

The accountant turned to Harold Shaw. "We're in terrible need of a tax deduction. Give him the best truck you have."

And that's how Enoch Olson ended up driving off the lot with a spanking brand-new, two-and-a-half-ton, red, flatbed truck.

Then came time for SpringHill's first campers. There were about 250 of them, and they hailed from Lydia Children's Home, an orphanage in Chicago. These were kids who had no family, no one who wanted them, no hope.

Enoch knew those young, forsaken souls needed to come to SpringHill. But the need went both ways. SpringHill needed those kids just as badly. As a fledgling camp, the surrounding community wasn't exactly receptive to sending their precious cargo to an unfamiliar place with so many other tried-and-true options available. For SpringHill, those orphans were the only kids they could get to come to a brand-new camp. The kids with no hope represented the only hope for SpringHill's future. God was using this symbiosis to set the tone for the kind of miracle that would be a part of SpringHill's legacy.

Enoch wanted to make those kids feel special, to have a really a cool and unique experience. Being a creative sort, he envisioned unusual housing for SpringHill including the idea that it would be fun if kids could sleep in covered wagons.

Enoch set to work recruiting churches and volunteers to build covered wagons that would hold five campers and a leader. And within days of the children's arrival from Chicago, the volunteers delivered, on flatbed trucks, all these covered wagons. Enoch arranged them in their places, installed campfire rings, marked hiking trails—the whole works, all the things that kids would want to do there. And in that first summer at SpringHill, from the slums of Chicago in an orphanage one night to a camp in northern Michigan where they slept in covered wagons, those kids who thought no one wanted them found camaraderie, they found hope, and they felt the grace of God.

I'm just as amazed as I was that first day I joined the ministry at SpringHill twenty years ago, when I walk around the camp among kids pouring out of the airplane and cabooses and stockade forts we have as housing. Over the course of my career here, we've enjoyed phenomenal growth and now serve 55,000 overnight and day campers in Michigan, Indiana, Illinois, Ohio, Georgia, Iowa, Kentucky, Tennessee, and Wisconsin, and partner with more than 500 churches and other allies. Our innovative approach helps children find God not only in quiet contemplation and formal prayer but also in canoeing on a lake, remembering that peace is there in the silence, when God whispers. Or while riding horses on country trails. Or while braving an outdoor high-ropes course. Or, yes, even on a zipline.

Some might think that what we've built here is just circumstantial, a result of dumb luck. Here at SpringHill, we know it's divinely inspired. We stand where we are because God gave Enoch a vision of what a Christian camp could be. Enoch ran with that vision and made it a reality. This vision has not only propelled SpringHill; it has influenced Christian camping all over the world.

Hope. Fun. Faith. For us, experience = everything.

That's The SpringHill Way.

CHAPTER ONE

God in All Things

"Start children off on the way they should go, and even when they are old they will not turn from it." —Proverbs 22:6

Mitigating Fear with Faith

- Fear and uncertainty are emotions we all wrestle with. Yet when we are afraid to take that next step in life, how do we cope? What tools are at our disposal?

- We often find ourselves thanking God for our blessings in life, but do we turn from Him when the journey gets difficult?

- If we believe God created everything, then it stands to reason that He is involved in everything. How do we strengthen our ability to find God in all aspects of our lives?

Would you ever think in a million years that you could learn some of the biggest spiritual lessons of your life on a zipline? Well, believe it or not it happens all the time at SpringHill. One of the stories that comes to mind is of a middle-school girl describing her experience at SpringHill. She had been a regular for years, and I just sort of casually asked her one day what it was that kept her coming back to SpringHill.

Very seriously, she said, "Every time I come to SpringHill, I encounter God. I have an experience with God and my faith grows."

And so I pressed her: "What exactly is it that happens every time?"

"You know," she said, "it just happens when we're doing camp stuff."

I smiled as she elaborated. "Like this last summer, I was on our zipline and I had been struggling ... should I really trust Jesus? I mean, really trust Him with my life? And then we go on the zipline and the leaders talk about how, for us to go down the zipline, we have to trust the cable that goes across the lake, trust the harness that we're in. We have to trust the pulleys that will go down the cable. We have to put our trust in them. If we don't do that and we don't take the step off the platform, we'll never get to the end. We'll never get across the lake. But it requires this trust."

"So what happened?" I asked.

"The leaders said ... it's the same with Jesus. We need to trust Him. We need to be able to step out with Him and know that He has us, holding onto us so that we won't fall. So I stepped off the platform, went down, and got to the end of the zipline, and I realized, yeah, this is what I need to do with Jesus. I need to trust Him just like I trusted the cable and the harness and everything else that comes down the zipline."

That's SpringHill, in that young girl, in that moment. That experience for her describes the integration of faith and fun, creating something altogether new and exciting, an activity that transforms into an extremely impactful, spiritual moment.

We used to talk about SpringHill as a place, a place on an old Shetland pony farm in mid-Michigan, where an ancient farmhouse was the first dining hall, where an abandoned fish hatchery existed. But over the years, we realized SpringHill really wasn't a place at all. SpringHill is an experience. Yes, we may have a way of doing, of creating experiences, but it really is about what God does in kids' lives.

We believe in The SpringHill Experience because we are so much more than a ministry or a summer camp. We have a way to connect kids with Jesus. I didn't invent this, but I did give it articulation, and life, and also built it into an organization, from being a kind of tribal, organic thing to being much more conscious and thoughtful and deliberate about leveraging our resources to grow and expand, to spread the word of Jesus to more children.

It's incredibly gratifying—and humbling—for me to take on the weighty responsibility of helping young people discover and become all God has created them to be in Christ, so they're able to do all that God has called them to do in Christ. I consider this *my* calling, and, to me, it calls to mind the critical difference between making a living and making a life.

There are lots of different ways to learn something. At SpringHill, we want kids to learn about Jesus, but we also want them to experience the truth of the Gospel through doing something they will remember for the rest of their lives. Kids hear about Jesus throughout their week, they see Jesus through our leaders, and they experience Jesus by doing things that require courage, community, trust, and faith.

We believe those are the things that kids will be able to refer back to time and time again on their spiritual journey, and we believe that's what makes the difference. Experience is everything at SpringHill, and we know it's what kids take back home with them after a week with us.

When kids encounter God outside church on Sunday, away from their parents, aside from their "normal" lives, faith and spirituality start to become much more real. It's not that our activities are flashy or state of the art. It's that they stick with kids because they stand out from the norm. It's simple, but it's highly impactful.

When kids go home, it's our hope they start to see God all around them and are able to apply what they learned at SpringHill to their everyday lives. From how they interact with teammates to how they approach bullies in the hallway, because kids saw Jesus in their counselors, heard about Him throughout their week, and experienced Him through our activities, they have a much more holistic perspective of what being a Christ follower means in this world.

Every day I see it and hear it all around me, and every day I'm all the more convinced that kids don't just go through SpringHill; they let SpringHill go through them. Every day I encounter the profound and the precocious. I can't help but smile when I reflect on what Ny'Asia Powell, age eleven, said:

> I was really excited about doing the Eurobungy again this summer at SpringHill. I really like jumping high. I feel like when I jump high on the Eurobungy that it feels like God is catching me, and when I go back down, He is washing away my sins. My counselors were really funny and super awesome! During my week at SpringHill, I learned that I can trust in God no matter what. It doesn't matter the situation you find yourself in, you can trust Him. After SpringHill, I want to apply what I learned about God and in the stories to my life and my family.

Like so many other SpringHill campers, Ny'Asia tells of taking risks, stretching limits, heeding Jesus's words repeated in variants of "Be not afraid."

What Is *The SpringHill Way?*

Enoch Olson, SpringHill's founding director and leader for many years, stressed encountering Jesus in all camp activities, and that's exactly what we do to this day. Our counselors, whom we refer to as our summer leaders, act as older siblings to kids through their excitement and passion for sharing their love of Christ with young people. Our staff is trained to look for "teachable moments" that apply God's teaching to everyday life and camp activities, and they become young mentors, friends, and confidants.

Our counselors are the ones who really make all the difference at SpringHill. Far more than anyone else in our ministry, they embody The SpringHill Way to their charges. Our college-age counselors are all vetted, committed to Christian values, and eager to share the Word in an uncommonly effective way. They are specially trained to impart God-centered values without being preachy or judgmental or overly pious, for young children and teens are still forming their ideas about faith. We take great pride in our counselors' ability to gently segue into coaxing youngsters to recognize the Lord's presence in their lives. The counselors are trained to employ the Socratic method, enabling the youth to discern God's presence on their own.

We designed SpringHill to have fairly low ratios of counselors to kids, both for our day camps and our overnight camps. Even when we do retreats, we have that same kind of requirement. In fact, we've created the program around those counselors, those leaders, being with their kids twenty-two hours a day.

One counselor might be a lifeguard for example, one might

work at archery, one might work at arts and crafts. We hired additional staff to spearhead those activities so the counselors and their respective charges can stay together.

The beauty of this design is that throughout the week, when kids and counselors are doing things together, maybe on the zipline or riding horses or participating in water activities, they're all doing these things *together*. Those shared experiences become a key part of community building. And when we integrate faith with fun in those activities, not only do they have that shared experience of doing the activity together but also the shared experience of discovering that the activity offers an opportunity for a faith lesson, essentially building a small community in Christ all through the week.

On the very first day of camp we have a relationship-building and trust-building exercise for the counselors and their kids, which we call GWAPS (games with a purpose). This is where they get to know each other and kind of set the culture of their cabin and their group, getting an idea of what it's all going to look like. We train our leaders on how to manage things that may come up with kids who are bullying or mistreating others, or when conflicts occur. And we have a whole group of support leaders who are there to help out in those situations, really just facilitating the kids to embrace not only SpringHill, but each other, and making sure that bond is reflected in the entire community.

Cell phones are off limits during our campers' time at SpringHill. There's no constant checking of social media to distract them from Christ's message. Instead, the children find faith in fun and building friendships. Surprisingly, they wouldn't want it any other way. But don't take my word for it. Emily Walsworth, one of our high-school students, couldn't have said it any better:

I love SpringHill because it forces you to socialize with people. We don't have our phones, so our only source of communication is the people that are in the same cabin as us. It's so refreshing to be able to have real conversations without worrying about looking through my Instagram feed or if the person I'm talking to has more followers than I do, because at SpringHill it doesn't matter.

Instead, she is frolicking and racing and tumbling and jumping, and even in the quiet moments, the young people at SpringHill—like Emily—are connecting with God. After campers overcome their fears and doubts about finishing the challenge course, complete with rock-climbing walls and high ropes, counselors are right there to chat about how campers can encounter Jesus in the activities. Herein lies the essence of The SpringHill Experience: young Christians growing in their journey of faith and hope and love through Christ in every activity, every day at camp.

"My favorite part of camp has to be when we are debriefing after an activity. It helped me learn more about Christ, but it also was very interesting, and a great way to show me how to start putting Christ in everything I do." —Leah

---

For counselors, camp leaders, and SpringHill kids, The SpringHill Experience means a community of infectious joy, and with that kind of love for God, miracles can happen.

Not long ago I was doing a tour at one of our overnight camps with an investment banker. His daughter was a regular at camp, and he wanted to see what SpringHill was all about. This is a guy who has just flown in from China on his private jet, and wields a firm that invests in companies all over the world.

So I was giving him the royal treatment, showing him what we do. We happened to be in the gym when I spotted one of our summer leaders approaching.

"Do you have a moment to talk?" he asked.

Of course, whenever something like that happens, I think, *Uh-oh, what's wrong?*

This was awkward because the investor just stared back and forth from me to the young man. I'm sure he was thinking exactly what I was thinking.

"I've just got to tell you," the young leader began as I held my breath. "This is my second summer. I've never had this happen this way. I just want you to know. I just need to share what happened when we were all at the campfire last night."

The investor and I were all ears as he relayed his tale. "My group of middle-school boys and I were just talking and sharing about the day … and the entire cabin group … made commitments to Christ."

The investor broke into a grin as the young man continued. "It was like they all said, 'Look, this is real. We need to do something with this.' It was just overwhelming that my whole cabin made these decisions."

SpringHill sets the stage for impactful and life-changing experiences to happen in an instant.

SpringHill sets the stage for impactful and life-changing experiences to happen in an instant.

And up the chain it goes, even with our leaders. Every summer, we have counselors whose lives are transformed, who literally change their career plans based on their experiences here at SpringHill. After their work with our kids, it never fails that some decide to become a teacher, embark on a career in special education, or go to work with the poor.

So although SpringHill is designed for smaller group experiences, we do have these larger group experiences as well, experiences that affect the larger community as a whole. And I think that's been beneficial for our kids because it helps them see that it's not just their small group, but that they're part of a larger group. And so when they leave SpringHill, they understand that even though they may have this close group of friends or these people that they're connected with, this faith group, they're actually a part of a much larger community, whether it's church, or the neighborhoods they live in, or the cities they're a part of, or the schools they go back to, and they have a responsibility in that.

To sum up The SpringHill Experience and the lingering effects on the community, allow me to share one of our most remarkable stories about a church partner of ours in suburban Detroit. It's a fairly wealthy suburban area that sponsors a scholarship for about thirty or forty kids from a local trailer park community. Almost all the kids and parents from that community are immigrants from Central and South America. So during the two weeks of day camp, this church picked these kids up in vans every morning, brought them to the church for day camp, and brought them home each evening.

By the end of the week, as they were being driven home, the kids were asking the church staff if they could continue to come back to camp, back to SpringHill. Well, SpringHill was done, but they meant they wanted to come back to *church*. So the church staff started picking these kids up every Sunday morning and bringing them to the children's program at the church.

And then came the ripple effect. Once the kids started attending church, guess who else wanted to attend church? The family, the parents, and the rest of the community. So these immigrant families from South America and Central America started coming to this predominantly white, suburban, wealthy church. Well, the church staff immediately figured out that most of them didn't speak English very well, so they started offering English as a second language for this community.

Now *everybody* from this community became involved in the church. And it all happened as an outcome of the kids' experience at SpringHill.

But that's not all.

When school finally started that September, Bob, the senior pastor of the church, received a phone call from the elementary school principal who serves that community. This woman was, apparently, not a Christian at all but called the church and asked to speak with Bob.

"I'm calling because I need to know what happened to some of my students this summer," she said. "There's a whole bunch of students from this trailer park community, and they're all wearing SpringHill tie-dye shirts."

That's one of the things that happen when kids go to the day camp: they make a SpringHill tie-dye shirt. It's kind of a SpringHill thing, and the kids feel a great sense of camaraderie wearing them. Evidently, these kids had been wearing their SpringHill tie-dye shirts to school.

"What the heck is SpringHill?" she demanded.

So Bob explained to her about SpringHill, and the church, and the effect it had on the families in the community. But by then Bob had grown concerned about the principal's tone.

"Is everything ... alright?" he asked.

"Alright?" she repeated. "Everything couldn't be better. They seem like different kids. They're better students, they're paying attention, they're better behaved. They're more focused than they were a year ago. And you know what, Bob?"

Bob was pleasantly flabbergasted. "What?"

"Next summer you can have all my students."

The ripple effect of God's hand in all we do exceeds what we could ever plan.

That's the kind of fascinating spillover we see so often with families, whose lives change as well because they see such a dramatic change in their kids. At the end of each week we talk with our kids about how they will be different when they go home, not just that they will *believe* differently but also how what they experienced at SpringHill will change their lives.

> **The ripple effect of God's hand in all we do exceeds what we could ever plan.**

"This was my fifth summer at SpringHill. This summer was different than all the rest. I found God. My counselors and the girls in my cabin really showed me what true love was and what it meant to be a real Christian. This year I accepted Jesus into my heart on the New Fro basketball courts. It was the best decision I have ever made and my life is already starting to change for the better. I'm so excited to go back next summer!" —Madeline

---

Even after two decades at SpringHill, I still marvel at how the young people find Christ not only in quiet contemplation and Bible study but just as likely on the zipline, or when overcoming fears to complete the challenge course, or talking quietly at the evening campfire about God's presence in their day. If the church is the hope of the world, then children are the hope of the church, just as in those early days at SpringHill with the orphan kids from Chicago. And the children of SpringHill, generations of them now, give me hope. For we're a generation away from transforming the world as we know it, either for the good or for the bad. Today the choice is ours about how we should raise our children and what our world will look like tomorrow.

SpringHill is nondenominational (though the mostly Midwestern camp has more Catholics than any other denomination), but I think of one of my favorite sayings of the Jesuit Catholic order is "Find God in all things."

For two decades, I have applied that maxim daily, as it forms the underpinnings of The SpringHill Experience.

Reflections on God in All Things

The safest route in life is to have low expectations for yourself and others, to set only achievable goals (or maybe no goals at all), and to take the proven path. The safe route assures that you are—safe. But it almost never brings you to a place that's meaningful or makes a true difference.

Should this type of safety be our overarching goal? Is it possible to make a real difference in the world and in the lives of others and, at the same time, take the safe path? The answer is a resounding *no*.

Reaching higher is always a risky proposition, but with risk comes great returns. Safety instead of risk means a life with no lasting rewards, only temporary comfort. Our son, Mitch, spent two years as a student at the United States Naval Academy (USNA). As a plebe, he was required to memorize the following quote from Teddy Roosevelt: "Far better is it to dare mighty things, to win glorious triumphs, even though checkered with failure ... than to rank with those poor spirits who neither enjoy nor suffer much, because they live in a gray twilight that knows not victory nor defeat."

And there's a reason all midshipmen are required to memorize this statement. The USNA, where young people dare to put themselves in an incredibly competitive and pressure-filled environment and be subject to discipline, hardship, and a career requiring them to take an oath to defend the Constitution of the United States with their life entails a huge risk. But the potential reward is incredible, for the midshipmen and, more importantly, for others and for the world.

So here's the bottom line: we're given only one life to live on this earth, one life to have an eternal impact on others, one life to explore this planet, and one life opportunity to change the world. We can choose to avoid the risks of trying to reach higher, but we can never live free of all risks, because when we take the safe route, we take the significantly bigger risk of living in that gray twilight where there is neither loss nor any lasting reward.

We all feel compelled, at one point or another, to move in a new direction, to take a monumental step, or make a key decision even though it feels risky and uncertain. As our SpringHill kids do, do you put aside your fears and trust in God with the big changes in *your* life? Remember children learn by example. How can you make your faith in God, which means taking risks, more a part of *their* everyday life? How do believing and living out those beliefs relate?

CHAPTER TWO

Our Secret Sauce

"Your word is a lamp for my feet, a light on my path." —Psalm 119:105

Knowing Who You Are and Your *Why*

- God created each one of us to be unique for a reason.

- Identity is one of the most important things we will ever discover. Have you really thought about who you are? What drives you? What motivates you? What makes you different form everyone else?

- We all have goals in life, yet do we know how to achieve them? Are you guided by just your desires, or do you have a set of core values steering you?

So what exactly is it that makes SpringHill different? What are the factors that all come together to make our ministry successful, not only within the gridlines of an Excel document or reflected on a balance sheet or touted in a year-end audit, but in the hearts and minds of our board members, staff, leaders, stakeholders, church partners and other community affiliations, the communities we serve, and the kids we host year after year?

In other words, what's our secret sauce?

A unique way of blending faith and fun is part of it. It's certainly a key ingredient in defining SpringHill as what it is, kind of like the special blend of herbs and spices that go into your favorite chili. It's what gives it that signature flavor that makes you hungry just thinking about it. Yet spices alone do not a chili make. There's more, so much more, that goes into crafting the perfect, mouth-watering bowl, from the host of ingredients in exactly the right measure and added to the pot at precisely the right moment, the cooking time and temperature, and the cooling time, down to the minutia of the kind of kettle or pot used, whether to stir with a wooden spoon or a metal one, even the storage strategy. Then, of course, we can't forget our signature spice mixture.

Chili can be a serious business. There are infinite combinations of ingredients and factors at play that yield endless chili recipes all over the world, and yet we all have our favorites. And you strike gold when you find a recipe that everyone seems to love. But what if that one special chili recipe that everyone knows and loves was created organically, intuitively, by a master chef with just a dash of this and a sprinkle of that, a few braised carrots here and a dollop of sour cream there? And what if you had to recreate that exact chili for a party of very special guests four hundred miles away, with no specific recipe to follow? That's a frightening thought, right?

Leaving our chili analogy to simmer for a moment, that's exactly what I had to do within my first few years of working at SpringHill.

Divinely Guided

Much in the way Enoch's involvement at SpringHill was what we like to think of as preordained, so, too, was mine. My wife, Denise, and I met while attending Central Michigan University, and during one of our summer breaks, Denise applied for a really great job at the university but was chosen as an alternate. In the meantime, some friends of ours had been telling us about their experiences as campers and later as counselors at this cool place called SpringHill. With her summer now wide open, Denise decided to become a camp counselor and, even to this day, recalls how transformative that single summer was in her life.

At the time, I had an internship at a company in Grand Rapids, and because she obviously couldn't leave her charges, I would head her way on the weekends, to a sleepy little town called Evart, Michigan, where I would spend time and hang around the camp with her. Over time, I got to know the staff at SpringHill, including Enoch and his wife, Joan, and their son, Mark, who was the program director. In the years that followed, Denise and I ended up growing very close to the Olsons, becoming ambassadors and supporters for SpringHill because we really connected with their approach and believed in their mission.

Fast-forward a bit to the mid-1990s. Ever the entrepreneur, I had a few business ventures rolling along at the time. I loved the thrill of owning my own company and being instrumental in watching it develop and expand, but as time wore on, I realized it just wasn't enough. Something was missing. Money has never been one of my motivators. In hindsight, I can see how God had known my path and helped me navigate it long before I knew it. I was extremely passionate about the scriptures, theology, and ministry. I had been a volunteer leader for Young Life, an organization I'd been involved with for fourteen years. I had developed a love of learning, teaching, coaching, and nurturing the spirits of others to help them become better leaders and followers of Christ, eager to share His word.

I suppose, being young and naïve, I thought I could feed my passion for serving others by launching scores of multimillion-dollar businesses and donating tons of money and free time to worthy causes, and all would be good and right in the world. But as any good entrepreneur knows, start-ups require every ounce of your time and talent. At the end of the day, I simply had nothing left to give.

By then, Mark Olson had taken over the role as president of SpringHill. Both of us were married, both of us had four kids, and our families spent a lot of time together. We vacationed together, shared our struggles, our dreams; it was one of those friendships you never forget. Mark and his father had created not just a place but an experience at SpringHill, an experience that was both revolutionary and extremely popular. The ministry had finally grown to the point where it was decided to open a second camp in southern Indiana. Mark wanted to travel to Indiana and spearhead the effort, but the Michigan board was reluctant to lose him if he didn't provide a replacement for himself in Michigan.

That's when he asked me to take over as the Michigan SpringHill director. Needless to say, I was both humbled and thrilled. Business with a purpose, the two things I loved.

And then tragedy struck.

During the summer opening of our Indiana camp, Mark was feeling ill. He would go through these bouts of pain and sickness, and so, for weeks, he went back and forth to the hospital, trying to get to the bottom of what was wrong. By September doctors had diagnosed him with an aggressive form of leukemia. Nine months later, Mark passed away.

Not only had I lost a dear friend, but SpringHill had lost its leader, its heart. I had been working very closely with the board and running both camps in the midst of all this. Little did I know, however, that the board had devised a succession plan long before Mark had ever got sick. And that succession plan was me.

Zero to sixty: I had gone from being the Michigan camp director to being the president of SpringHill, overseeing two camp ministries 450 miles apart, with no director in Michigan to fill my shoes. And with the second summer upon us for our Indiana site, not a week into the season the Indiana director let me know that was to be his last year at the post.

Somehow, some way, with God's grace, we were able to survive that summer, but by the fall, I was tired. I had doubts. I was afraid. And so I packed a bag and headed to Crystal Mountain Resort in northern Michigan for a short getaway, just to think about things. I needed to reflect and reexamine, to connect with my faith, way out in God's country, surrounded by the dazzling blue waters of Lake Michigan, the majestic Sleeping Bear Dunes, and the endless forests of white pine hemming in the quaint towns scattered throughout the area.

It was in one of those quiet moments, when all you can hear are the wind and the sound of your own breathing, that I asked God, "Why do you have me in this job? I'm no Mark Olson."

And not long after, I had my answer: if God had wanted Mark Olson in that job, he'd still be in it.

That was an incredibly freeing moment for me. I realized then, in that quiet contemplation, that I was uniquely qualified to not only maintain what SpringHill was, but help it grow to become all it could be. By harnessing my business and entrepreneurial background, I could build teams, figure out the right formula, and bottle the essence of The SpringHill Way so it could be replicated anywhere in the world.

God has a plan for each and every one of us, above and beyond what we could possibly anticipate.

Well, that summer while Mark was sick, I didn't really spend much time at the camp in Indiana, so during my first summer as the president of SpringHill, I spent half my time there

> God has a plan for each and every one of us, above and beyond what we could possibly anticipate.

to get myself acquainted with all the practices and procedures. And with every passing week I thought, *This isn't* SpringHill.

I rallied the staff members I trusted, folks who ran our programs, and consultants who knew SpringHill intimately. They all agreed. What was happening in Indiana might have been a Christian camp, but it certainly wasn't SpringHill.

That fall, I asked the board about the direction of the Indiana camp. After all, who was I to judge the board's decision if they had a different intention with the second property? They confirmed, however, that the intent for growth and expansion was to replicate exactly what had been created in Michigan. When I presented them the evidence that Indiana was a far cry from SpringHill, they gave me an assignment.

"You need to articulate what it means to be SpringHill," they said.

I had to recreate the chili everyone loved without knowing the exact recipe. So I called upon those who'd been involved with SpringHill, those who had tasted our special sauce, and ask them what ingredients they tasted. We did focus groups with stakeholders around the Midwest, from Grand Rapids to Indianapolis, to find out what made SpringHill SpringHill. And what we began to realize was that SpringHill wasn't a place; it was an experience. In fact, we had named our Indiana camp something totally different because we had it in our heads all along that SpringHill was a place.

So we put together a team of people, including Enoch, and digested all of the input. We concluded that one of the main things that made The SpringHill Experience what it was rested in the fact that although we were a Christian camp, in terms of theological truth, we majored on the majors. In other words, we'd always avoided those doctrinal and theological points that have been controversial and divided the church over the years, which in turn really opened the door for us to have all kinds of kids and all kinds of families.

We don't baptize campers or do Communion or Eucharist because we want to be respectful of everyone's individual beliefs. But we haven't watered down or washed out the Gospel, the Good News, either. What we do is focus on the fundamentals, the core of the Gospel. What that's done for us is create this sense of unity, of embracing *all* kids and universally accepting all Christian core beliefs. So we realized that kind of majoring on the majors is really an important part of our secret sauce, and it came right from the very beginning of SpringHill.

"I learned at camp that Jesus really, really wants to have a relationship with us and you don't have to be perfect for Jesus. He loves us the way we are, but wants us to follow him and be like him. My favorite verse in the Bible is Ephesians 2:8. It says, 'Your salvation doesn't come from what you do; it's God's gift.'" —Sammie

Enoch and the churches that started this whole ministry back in 1969 decided to major on the majors, not to advance a specific doctrine. So it always had this nondenominational, or interdenominational, feel to it: prayer, majoring on the majors, and uniting around the things that bind us together, not around the things that divide us. Our curriculum is pretty orthodox, pretty basic. It's really more about how we communicate it and the context in which we create the communication.

The Heart of SpringHill

What ended up coming out of our careful consideration and reflection was a unique set of four core values: contagious joy, relational focus, adventurous faith, and holy discontent.

1. **Contagious joy:** creating life-transforming experiences by combining faith and fun, innovation and the hope of the Gospel.

2. **Relational focus:** working in the context of personal, loving, and caring relationships. This is why we create these small communities and have different housing areas within SpringHill. We want to be creative, but we also want to create a sense of identity within those small communities. There's something about the power of that small community that really allows kids to hear and experience and see so they get to see Christ in the lives of their leaders because they're all connected through their small community for the week.

3. **Adventurous faith:** leaving room for God to work, being open to taking risks, knowing that He can do immeasurably more than we can imagine. This is the more obvious ingredient I opened the chapter with: this idea that through our activities, we're teaching

campers to trust God in their lives, and that we have to take those steps of faith and trust and can't control everything in the world.

4. **Holy discontent:** always striving to grow in Christ through professional curiosity, continuous improvement, and professional and personal sanctification. This really is reflected in Enoch Olson's masterplan of creating a camp that he could rearrange and move around. That really is a key part of who we are. We are always asking ourselves if we can do something better, How do we fulfill our mission better? How do we reach kids, engage kids, at a better level?

Interestingly, we don't just apply these core values to our campers' experiences, but to ourselves as well. Again, it goes back to our founding director, Enoch Olson. He was a man of great faith and expected to see God do miraculous things, not only for SpringHill and within SpringHill but for kids all over the world. To that end, we've done things and continue to do things that push us outside our comfort zone because we, too, believe this ministry is bigger than us.

For example, we started our day camp program in 2006. Immediately, we got pushback from people. Why are you doing that? That's not SpringHill. SpringHill's a place. And we said no, SpringHill's an experience. Even a few board members and constituents thought we were nuts. We tried it anyway ... and it started to grow. Then it just took off like wildfire. Well, word got around, not just around the Midwest but also around the country and—literally—around the *world!* No one else was doing what we were doing.

Suddenly, we're getting these phone calls and were faced with the opportunity for SpringHill to reach more kids than we had ever imagined. So what did we do? We made the decision, leaning on our core value of adventurous faith. "Look, this isn't ours," we said.

"None of this is really ours. We're just stewards of it. And if we can entrust to other organizations around the world what we've learned from doing day camps, we can have an impact on more kids than we can through what we do by ourselves. So we started sharing this know-how, and today, quite literally, there are tens of thousands of kids around the world who have had a day-camp experience like the one at SpringHill that we helped launch.

The adventurous faith part is that we were a for-profit in that endeavor, and we were supposed to be trying to make money at it. The last thing you do is give away your best new program or product to your competitors. But we frankly acknowledged that the world is full of kids. We were going to help others do what we do. And we never charged for it. We have consulted, worked with, and helped foster these programs because we believe that the mission and the cause of Christ are more important than SpringHill's mission.

Outcomes

And the more we thought about it, the more we dissected our secret sauce, we found that the way we live out our four core values can be described by the following six components:

1. **God immersed:** recognizing that it is God through Christ who works to change the lives of young people, not our programming and planning.

2. **Community focused:** everything at SpringHill happens within small communities that facilitate and enhance relationships.

3. **People:** inspired, trained, and professional staff and volunteers who fulfill our mission and vision in alignment with our core values.

4. **Embracing:** creating a welcoming place for all kinds of young

people, regardless of where they are spiritually, physically, emotionally, or socioeconomically.

5. **Innovative:** specifically designing our programs, facilities, and activities to be creative, relevant, fun, and challenging experiences that kids typically do not have.

6. **Integrated:** making no distinction between faith and fun to help kids discover spiritual truth inside everyday experiences.

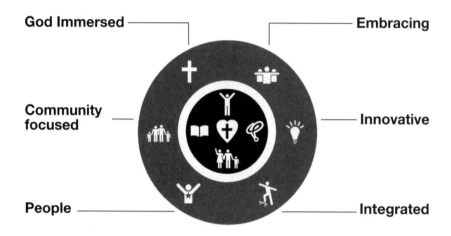

Through these core values, and the accompanying six components, remarkable things begin to happen. For one, SpringHill kids gain independence. They are challenged to think for themselves, to make good decisions, not by being lectured or chastised but through examples of Christian living all around them. We'll push them, gently, but convincingly enough to overcome fears by confronting them and developing trust. This, of course, builds self-confidence.

Additionally, they will develop character. Decisions at such critical junctures in their young lives can make or destroy their futures. We challenge children to give thanks always for abundant blessings, to discern the good spirits from the dark ones, and follow the light. We teach them to have a positive attitude, looking for the light even when God seems distant or when seized by fear or anxiety.

Next, SpringHill campers have the opportunity to hone their social skills. Perhaps more than at many less personable camps, SpringHill engages kids in conversation with leaders as well as fellow campers. And talk they do but not about what's on Instagram or TV. I'm astonished, at times, to hear how much they grasp at such a young age about the lessons that matter most. The kids learn to converse articulately while building interpersonal skills through real-time, face-to-face interaction with their peers and counselors, who take on a big sister or big brother role at camp.

While at SpringHill, our campers will make friends and build relationships, many of them blossoming into lifelong friends. The young people build relationships on solid foundations of trust and camaraderie with classmates and counselors through small-group time, the vast array of camp activities, around the campfire and meals, and in one-on-one chats with counselors or between campers.

And lastly, they learn to become leaders who influence others. Every child not only follows examples of leaders and fellow campers but takes on a leadership role at camp in group activities. This builds confidence and plants the seeds for leadership in a lifetime worthy of emulation.

When you understand those four core values and the six components we use to execute them, it makes sense why we do things the way we do, what we call The SpringHill Way. And these values truly *are* our core. They aren't something I brought to SpringHill personally; they've been with us since the very beginning.

In fact, we recruit and we screen against our core beliefs presented in those majors, as well as against those four core values. We only align ourselves with people who can live those values, truly. What that measure does is allow us to end up with a team of people, not only our team of staff and the people we hire in the summer, but also donors and board members and volunteers who line up with those four core values.

So that's our secret sauce. And it really is the tangible expression of those values that we hold dear, and those beliefs that we hold in our hearts to be true.

Reflections on Our Secret Sauce

"The whale that spouts first gets harpooned first" was one of the first things I learned in 1984 as I started in the management training program at Steelcase, Inc. A quote attributed to its then CEO and chairman, Bob Pew.

The message was clear: we shouldn't talk about how good we are as a company. We just needed to demonstrate it through our superior products, service, and value. The need to "spout" indicated more serious issues, issues that would eventually lead to being "harpooned."

Being understated was a strong value of Steelcase's and it permeated the entire company's culture. It's a value that continues to influence my career and, as a result, influences SpringHill.

It's so integrated into my own values that I hadn't thought much about the quote until one day, late in July, I drove by this sports bar in a small town near Marion, Indiana.

The sign on the side of the building read, "Best Damn Sportsbar Period."

As I went by the front of the bar, I said to myself, "It doesn't look like the best one, period," and then I noticed the "For Sale" sign in the window, which confirmed my assessment of the place.

The owners surely hadn't gone through Steelcase's management training program. If they had, they'd have known not to spend money spouting off on signs. But instead, they would have invested that money and energy into the service and experience they provided their customers, with the result that they wouldn't have needed that final sign I saw in the window.

When we are fully aligned with our mission and core values, our successes speak for themselves. But just as SpringHill does, we, too, all need specific guiding principles in our lives, our own set core values. What are your core values? Have you ever considered writing them down and sharing them with your friends and family? How about with the children in your life? How does your devotion to God factor into them? Can you look more intentionally for the ways God is leading you on your journey? How can you help the children in your life see God working in their lives?

CHAPTER THREE

Camping in a Caboose: The SpringHill Experience

"Nevertheless, the one who receives instruction in the Word should share all good things with their instructor." —Galatians 6:6

Where Faith Meets Fun

- At SpringHill, we believe that experience = everything. Everything we do is geared around unique experiences that reinforce lessons about living a righteous life, with God forever at the center.

- What experiences can you recall from your younger years that shaped who you are and how you look at the world? Did fun and happiness play a role?

- How does experience define us? Can you think of a minor experience that had a life-changing impact? Think about a time when something fun changed the way you view the world.

I talked to a mom in the summer of 2017. Her son was a part of our experience for children in their late elementary-school years (fifth graders going into the sixth grade). Mom said her son had been to other day camps in the past, but they were now taking the leap to an overnight camp. She said that her son had really struggled in school, struggled in feeling accepted among his peers, and social life was a challenge for him. She was extremely worried about her son participating in our overnight experience because it's immersive and close-knit, and she wouldn't be there to intervene, to rescue him from whatever might happen with the other kids.

I'd seen this fear played out a hundred times before. And as always, I knowingly and compassionately assured her that all would be well. Sure enough, a week later, she came to pick her son up. And not long after, I received a phone call.

Mom was in tears on the other end. "When I picked him up, it was the happiest I've seen him in a long, long time. And on the way home, I just asked him, 'Why was it so good? What was so good about this place?' And he said, 'Mom, they loved me and accepted me.' I asked, 'You mean the counselors?' He says, 'Oh yeah, them too. But it was the kids in my cabin.' Michael, he felt for the first time in his life he was part of a community, you know?"

There's no better remedy than feeling you belong somewhere.

> **There's no better remedy than feeling you belong somewhere.**

"One of my favorites was rock climbing. We talked about how, sometimes, you don't always make it, and each rock is like getting a step closer to God. God's like the rope that holds you up. Sometimes you have high and lows with your relationship with God and the actions that you do make your relationship with God. Camp helps my relationship with God because every day we will talk about Him and it's really fun!" —Katie

---

Yes, I did know. I knew very well. And I think when young people have that kind of transformative experience, it opens them up to the movement of God in their lives. They see how the world, how people, how peers and mentors and friends *should be*.

This mother saw her son accepted and loved in a way that he wasn't experiencing at home or at school. I think that the idea of our community—of embracing all kids, of making room, of innovation, doing unique things that kids normally don't get to do, integrating faith and fun, all of it—leads to this place where God shows up. I truly think part of it is that God shows up in our kids' lives in different places. One kid might be struggling, socially, and suddenly feels accepted in his cabin community. Other kids might be struggling with trust and fear, and while going down the zipline, or climbing a rock wall, or riding a horse, they suddenly have a transformative moment.

> When young people have that kind of transformative experience, it opens them up to the movement of God in their lives. They see how the world, how people, how peers and mentors and friends *should be.*

> "My time here at camp was fun. The best part about it was the giant swing, because there is a feeling of being free up there. I related the activity to God by saying, 'When you go up there, you are holding on to the rope and as soon as you let that go, you're free and you fall.' So, is there something in your life that you are holding on to that you need to be letting go of? There was a situation in my life where one of my close friends died and that was really tough, but I let it go." —Dearis

Campfires always bring surprises, a-ha moments, quiet contemplation. You'll hear teenagers speaking articulately and eloquently about the life of David, the Kingdom of God, how David was created to be a king, how God called David to be a king and how Samuel anointed David. SpringHill kids always begin the day with the theme that God looks at our heart, and this becomes the theme for the rest of the day: God calls you and wants a relationship with you. The counselors ask, at campfires, where the kids experienced this truth in their day. When did they feel like David? Who was called by God? When did they receive God's personal invitation?

The SpringHill Experience

The first day of The SpringHill Experience, kids are immediately brought into their small group, which, for an overnight camp, is their cabin group. And immediately, the counselor begins connecting with them, getting to know them, encouraging each of them to know each other, already starting to set the tone.

Our counselors are young, passionate, fun role models who are open about their love for God and God's love for children. Our top goal is to integrate faith and fun throughout each day of camp, and counselors are always ready to deliver a life lesson during those fun activities. SpringHill kids are with the same counselors the entire week. This gives counselors the time to get to know each child and become emotionally invested in that child's life. A counselor's sole purpose is to build a genuine relationship with all campers and make sure they are well taken care of and included at SpringHill.

Our counselors, or summer leaders as we like to call them, also ensure that campers are never alone. They stay in the cabins with their charges and spend the whole day with the cabin groups, participating in activities and leading small group sessions. We have additional counselors who run activities during the day and stay with our kids at night to provide extra support both in the activities and in the cabins. This ensures that campers are never left alone and still get the individualized attention that they need.

Homesickness is not uncommon at SpringHill, usually because it's a child's first time away from home for an extended period of time. We are aware of this and love to care for and pray for each child who is having a difficult time being away from home. Most of the time, homesickness occurs right before bed, so our counselors are trained in how to anticipate and care for a lonely child.

"At first, I didn't do any of the activities because I was scared, but then I realized that I was having trouble trusting God to keep me safe." —Chris, Teen Service Team

---

We always have trained medical staff to manage a child's health-care needs. Our counselors go to great lengths to ensure campers receive the treatment and medications they require. Kids who take medication will receive the right dose at the right time, every day. And at every level, staff members are not permitted to be alone with kids. Campers and staff must always be within view of others or in groups of at least three. Additionally, we make it a point to help educate parents on how to keep their children safe.

While at SpringHill, kids are most influenced by their counselors. Part of our interview and hiring process examines candidates' relationship with God and how they communicate it to others. Our staff is committed to sharing their faith and is equipped to do so in a way that makes sense for groups of different ages, biblical knowledge, or religious background.

Now imagine being middle-school age and greeting the day with your new friends and counselor by your side, in one of our amazing housing options: Clarks Grant or Western Town, or perhaps, Meadowland Cabins: real log cabins that have electricity and are divided into three bedrooms with a common room in the center and a bathhouse nearby. Or Peaks, named for various mountain peaks throughout the United States, where housing units are designed with comfort in mind, boasting inside showers and facilities.

And then there is *The Provider*, a C-123K aircraft, one of the coolest housing units on property. *The Provider* is a real plane that flew in the Vietnam and Korean Wars and now rests peacefully at our Evart, Michigan, site. Or how about awakening in a caboose at SpringHill Junction, one of nine unique, restored cabooses that form the SpringHill Junction train line?

On that first morning, SpringHill kids enrolled in our overnight program are given the theme for the day, which really sets the tone for the running programmatic theme that is strategically echoed in activities and conversations throughout the course of the week. Next, they participate in a series of activities with their group, and at the end of each activity they engage in a debriefing exercise, all connected to their designated theme.

Each day, SpringHill kids will have study, or story time, and participate in small group discussions with their counselors. All children will be challenged to think for themselves and come home with a greater desire to pray and read the Bible. Our staff actually spends months working on an age-appropriate curriculum that will inspire and encourage kids of all ages to learn more about God and His love for His children.

"This week I've learned amazing Bible stories, had a great time at campfire, but most importantly, I'm now ready to be more committed to God and excited to put God in front of everything else. SpringHill was a week I will not forget." — Taylor

---

We believe that God gave us community to help us through challenges, which is why every activity at camp comes with an objective lesson. Campers will face challenges and adventures right alongside cabin mates and counselors. After all, we don't go through this life alone; we get to go on this adventure together!

From the heart-pumping zipline, to kayaking, canoeing, and stand-up paddle-

We don't go through this life alone; we get to go on this adventure together!

boarding, where campers learn how to navigate their way through the summer camp waters, and from The Gusher, a new twist on the waterslide, to our fifty-foot climbing wall, SpringHill summer camp spurs children to grow and mature, to gain independence.

"I got to ride a zipline, ride down a ginormous water slide, and fly off a blob! Not only did we get to do all this fun stuff, but we got to learn cool stuff about God. He loves even when we do bad things like lie to our parents." —Caleb

---

Our activities, however, are a mix of both high intensity and low intensity. Campers will experience high adventure, waterfront, and target sports activities as well as enjoy socially focused activities such as volleyball and battle bows. We know that teens tend to crave more interaction with their peers and high-energy situations in larger groups. That's exactly what they get at SpringHill. And they will be challenged to think for themselves and make good decisions. They will be challenged to overcome fears and try new things, thereby building self-esteem and confidence.

SpringHill offers children an environment where they are encouraged to interact and talk to other children and their counselors. This helps build interpersonal skills and takes children away from the computer screen and into real, face-to-face interaction with others. And we help develop young leaders, in small-group activities, to have an impact on the other campers.

Solo time in the morning introduces the Bible story of the day. Campers read this on their own and answer questions individually. Counselors then lead a brief small-group discussion. Around lunch time, the small group discusses the same story from the morning to provide another way for the campers to connect with the key characters and principles.

Club is a time of funny skits, a worship set with the band, and a dramatic performance. The performances present real-life issues for middle-school campers that are processed afterward in a small group. And every evening, we have a fun, epic event for all campers. This is a time to bring everyone together and pull off something big! Crud Wars is the tradition; think giant mud war with as many as 400 middle-schoolers.

"The short skits we would see before our small groups, both at focus and club, had strong messages that spoke to me. My understanding of how much he loves us, how much he thinks of us, how he is our father, our friend, our Savior, and so much more, grew so much. Seeing the words on the screen and getting a chance to dance, to sing, and to praise everything God has done for us is an amazing experience that I cherish every year. And of course, there is the correspondence between our activities and our walk with Christ, showing us in a more poetic sense, what we need to do, and where we need to put our faith." —Annie

---

If Walt Disney had built a Christian camp, I really believe it would have been SpringHill.

We don't ever want a kid to *not* experience SpringHill due to a family's inability to pay. To that end, we offer several convenient payment options, including monthly installments. We even have scholarships and financial assistance programs, which are made possible every year through generous gifts of individuals and organizations. In fact, we've never turned a kid away for financial reasons. We're determined to always find the money some way, somehow.

Equally as exciting as our overnight camping experiences are SpringHill's day camps. Over 130 local churches host SpringHill's day camps as an effective outreach program for their community. Day camps include small-group Bible teaching, high-energy large-group sessions, and adventure activities such as archery, bungee trampoline, camp songs, climbing wall, crafts, and more.

Innovation: Day Camp in Detroit

I think one of my favorite day camp stories is when we partnered with the Mack Avenue Community Church in the city of Detroit. The people who founded that church back in the mid-2000s had the notion to plant a church in a needy community, a community that was really struggling. They looked at all the demographics and all the information, and they ended up picking an impoverished community in Detroit, quite literally, the second poorest zip code in the country.

We connected with them, and soon began a partnership along with another church called Hope Community Church. During 2008, 2009, and 2010, at a time when all the pictures of Detroit blight were scattered on the news—abandoned homes, abandoned schools, even abandoned police stations—we started up one of our day camps. We actually used a vacant public school for the week, totally surrounded by abandoned homes. And one day, one of those homes actually collapsed. It just fell down. That moment served as a tangible representation of the blight and hope in the community we looked to serve.

The people at Mack Avenue told us they had been there for a number of years, and it had taken six months of relationship building before a family would even consider coming to the church. And so they had all these connection points out there, just trying to serve the community, yet having little success. But they said that when SpringHill's day camps came in, those six months almost immediately became "overnight." Those families on whom they had hoped to have an impact, once we served their kids, were immediately open to becoming engaged in the church and becoming part of that fellowship!

"I started going to Mack Avenue Community Church when I was five and the kids' ministry helped me learn why I'm alive and what Jesus did for me, and why He went on the cross: to take away my sins. Then I started going to SpringHill day camps and grew my relationship with God and learned more about who He really is." —Sarah

---

Yet the impact we had on the kids was even greater. One of the mothers told the church, afterward, about her conversation with her son on the last day of camp.

"Where are they going?" the little boy asked his mom as the summer leaders packed up.

"Well, it's Friday," Mom replied. "This is your last day, and then SpringHill has to go on."

"No! No, these are my friends, right? They're not going to leave me," he said.

"Well, yes, they're your friends," Mom said gingerly. "But they have to move on to go to other places for other kids."

The little boy thought about it for a moment before saying, "You know what? I'm gonna sneak into their suitcases. I'm gonna go with them!"

Our relationship with that church has been awesome. They serve their fellowship, they help start businesses, and they're doing other great things as well, as part of their holistic mission to the community. But they give credit to SpringHill's day camps as part of what helped them accelerate their ability to have an impact.

And I think that's a great picture of what we've been able to do at our day camps. We can take SpringHill and go to the second poorest zip code in the country, where, literally, abandoned homes are falling down around the camp, and we can have an impact on the lives of kids. In fact, that's one of my favorite places. I go every summer to Mack's day camp because I love the kids; I love what's going on. It's just a really cool story and cool partnership we have with them.

The SpringHill Experience is a universal language of God's love transcending all boundaries.

And again, we've found that this experience can happen anywhere, whether it's an inner-city Detroit neighborhood or in Indiana, surrounded by miles of farmland. We've done them in downtown Chicago. We've done them in rural communities, in small communities. We've done them in suburban areas. We've done them in the woods in our overnight camps.

The experience and the way we do it are transferable, and that, to me, is really part of the excitement of SpringHill. We can reach kids and serve families in ways that we never could if we were bound by the borders of a property.

That's The SpringHill Experience.

Reflections on Camping in a Caboose: The SpringHill Experience

Not too long ago I was at an automotive service run by a former SpringHill camper. When I picked up my car, I asked this SpringHill alum for a tour of his business. You see, I was not only interested in learning about his business, but, more importantly, I wanted to get a glimpse into the life of one of our former campers.

After the tour, we stood in the middle of his shop floor and talked about his life as a young entrepreneur. Our conversation drifted to SpringHill and reminiscing about those summers when his parents would drop him and his brothers off at camp. As we shared those memories together, I could see his eyes lighting up. That was when he said, "It's funny you're here and we're talking about camp because I was just recently thinking about my camp experiences. It's become clear to me just how important they were in my development as a person. I was a shy, quiet kid. But at camp I gained confidence to interact with others and build positive relationships."

Hearing him say this, while sitting in the middle of his impressive business, brought to life the reality I've built my vocation on: summer camp is an incredibly spiritual, emotional, and social building experience. Camp is one of those milestone moments when people's lives take a quantum step forward.

And this is why SpringHill is so committed to creating life-transforming experiences. We see no other short-term experience in the world that provides young people such a life-long payback as summer camp does. If there were, trust me, SpringHill would offer it in a New York minute. But there just isn't. There's no other experience that provides the breadth and depth of personal, long-term growth that summer camp does.

This means there is no better short-term investment, with such a life-long payback, that parents can make for the child they love than sending that child to a SpringHill camp this summer.

At SpringHill, we believe that experience is everything. Have you thought about the experiences *you* create, and how they relate to serving others, as well as serving God? What is the value of these kinds of experiences in your own life? What plans or intentional steps can you take to assure you have these kinds of experiences? Now think about the experiences you create for the children in your life. What are your hopes and dreams for them? What kinds of experiences do you want them to have? Do those experiences help shape their relationship with God?

CHAPTER FOUR

Journeys of Faith and Friendship

"And we know that in all things God works for the good of those who love Him, who have been called according to His purpose." —Romans 8:28

Building a Bridge to God and Others

- Our connection to others is critical on our personal journeys. What lasting friendships have you built to help you on your way though life?

- Our connection to God is also critical on our spiritual journeys. When did you really start to form that connection, and how has He helped you?

- Do our personal and spiritual journeys ever intersect? Have you ever needed someone to help you on your spiritual journey?

We had a young man who was in late elementary school and who first came to SpringHill as a camper. He was from the Flint, Michigan, area. He grew up in a home where faith and church were not a part of his life. But he had a friend who had signed up for SpringHill and invited him to come along.

When he came to SpringHill, he saw and felt the power of faith and Gospel for the first time, and it just overwhelmed him.

"There's something real about this," he said to his buddy.

He made a big decision at camp that first summer. From that point on, he became committed to SpringHill, and more importantly, committed to his journey of faith. So he came back to camp with his friend the next summer. And the summer after that. And the summer after that. When he grew old enough, he started to attend church on his own and really grew in his faith. Then he ended up going to Western Michigan University and got involved in one of the local campus ministries.

Without any family encouragement, he took the reins and went about his journey of faith on his own. He came back and worked for us one summer. He was an intern, and he did a really great job. It is interesting to note that when he graduated, he was recruited by a large international ministry to be an assistant to the president. He did that for a couple years and now is working for a global ministry. He's been with them at least ten years and is doing a great job. Today he's married with kids of his own. Yet his whole life trajectory all started with a friend asking him to go to SpringHill.

"I have been a Christian all my life but I never really felt that close to God. I was never really that comfortable praying out loud, but by the end of the week, I really enjoyed it. I now feel like I can actually have a conversation with God." —Anna

It's that kind of journey we spark, that kind of connection we build, that makes SpringHill, and my job, so special. We've always offered this place that embraces all kinds of kids, including kids who have totally different faith backgrounds, or no faith background at all. Here they can come and feel welcomed. We've created the type of ministry that a family can trust; they can invite friends and know these friends will not just hear the Gospel but be embraced and loved for who they are.

For us, it feels like a partnership with that family who invited this young man to the camp: we partnered with them to help them reach out to their family and friends. There's a partnership with the families we serve. There's an embracing.

I think the other thing about this story that I like is that we walked along with him. We weren't in his life every day as a local church would be, or perhaps another kind of ministry, but we were that one milestone every year in his life that became really important. He always knew he could come back and be part of SpringHill, always have that SpringHill Experience.

We hear, over and over again, kids saying, "I come back because this is a place where I experience Christ, and it gets me refocused."

We create an ongoing relationship in which our campers grow as people and in their faith. And if we are fortunate enough, we remain involved with them, helping them move into a career, always supporting them.

There are some ministries, similar to ours, that have a defined purpose of calling people into the ministry, but that's not what we're trying to do. We're trying to help people discover their purpose, discover who they are, and discover whatever it is God has called them to do.

There are always kids who meet at camp and have The SpringHill Experience together, kids who live very far apart and likely would never have a chance to interact. But every year, they come right back together as if no time at all has passed. It even happened to my oldest son. In his second year at SpringHill, he befriended a camper with special needs, a great kid, just lovable. He latched onto my son. And for about three or four years in a row, my son and my wife coordinated with the other boy and his mom, because her son wanted to be there with my son. They came back to camp together every year.

We see that with our high-school program, which we call Teen Service Teams (TST). Kids work together for two weeks, half camper and half staff. They might work in the kitchen, or in dining hall, or on the grounds, or cleaning. They work together and then they have fun together. It creates this incredible bond, so much so that it's kind of the inside joke that after your kids go, they will have all these reunions for years to come with a group of people they mopped the floors with. They might even meet two or three times a year for a weekend in somebody's home and catch up.

"Everyone here at SpringHill is positive and wants nothing more but to help, and strengthen your relationship with God. Here I feel safe, and filled with love and trust." —Hannah, Teen Service Team

---

Transformative Summers

We consider ourselves evangelical, but sometimes, that label creates a certain image in people's minds about who we are and what we are about, which isn't necessarily accurate. So here's a story that shows the God-immersed part of SpringHill, and how transformative a summer here can be.

It involves one of our high-school kids, a TST kid named Tom. He had been coming to SpringHill, our camp in Michigan, since he was a little boy. He came year after year. By this time, Tom was coming and doing the TST thing as a high-schooler, so he kind of transitioned into that next role. His counselor, his area director, and one of the staff leaders came up to me one morning.

"Hey, Michael," one of them said. "Tom wonders if he could talk to you."

I was a little nervous. "Is everything okay?"

He shrugged. "I don't know. Something happened last night at the campfire, I guess, and he'd like to share it with you."

We ended up meeting at a picnic table, Tom and myself, along with his counselor and area director. And so Tom went on to tell me that he had been coming to SpringHill for a long time. Every time he came to SpringHill, he felt he had an encounter with God, and each time, God changed him a little, changed his perspective, changed his view of things, and he grew in his faith.

He said that prior to that summer, he was all signed up to come, and he just knew he was going to have another one of those encounters with God.

"I was afraid," Tom said.

"Why?" I asked.

Tom drew in a breath. "Because I wasn't sure I would want to have another encounter. I thought seriously about not coming. But I knew I'd been coming every year, and I couldn't run away from this, so I came."

I knew whatever Tom felt, whatever encounter he was going to have with God, was going to be something really transformative for him. It was going to be significant, so much so that it scared him. The thing is we don't even talk in that language with the kids. Our curriculum is very straightforward and simple, nothing radical or forceful. But God does something at SpringHill.

"I just knew God was going to do something really crazy in my life," said Tom, "and it happened last night at campfire. And I want to tell you."

"So what happened last night at campfire?" I asked.

"Well," he said, "I'm Catholic. I've grown up Catholic. I'm part of the Catholic Church. And last night, when I was at campfire, God spoke clearly to me that I needed to become a priest. I needed to go into the priesthood."

For a young teenage guy to experience that kind of epiphany must have been overwhelming, and he needed some guidance. He asked my thoughts about what he should do, whom he should see. So I coached him through it. I told him to go see his priest. I told him that his Catholic church has a seminary and specialized schooling so he could obtain the proper theological training. That was a really sacred moment for me, and for SpringHill: we got to be part of that kind of life calling.

We are just an instrument in helping to facilitate God's plan for our lives.

And again, it probably sounds weird that an evangelical organization should take pride in that story about helping Catholics, but a good portion of our kids

We are just an instrument in helping to facilitate God's plan for our lives.

are Catholic, and we want them to grow in their faith. It's not really about being Catholic or Protestant for us. It's about our campers' relationship with Christ. And to be part of that, to see that transformation was truly a blessing.

But the truth is we didn't actually *do* anything. Everything at SpringHill is God's doing. You can't possibly manufacture that kind of a life-changing experience. Trying to coach a kid to become a priest would be the farthest thing from our counselors' minds.

It just happened. Kind of like the story of Brian Bennett.

Brian grew up in Michigan's thumb region, in a family that was in and out of ministry environments. Nearly thirty years ago, when he was ten, his parents saved up for the one and only summer camp he and his younger brother ever attended: a SpringHill overnight camp. This was of course early in our history, when we were still young and growing ourselves. We didn't have all the bells and whistles back then. Our activities were really basic in those days. Frog races down the grass hill where we hold now hold our rallies with thousands of people were a big deal. No zipline, no water slide, no warplane housing. But Brian remembers there was just something about the place that was contagious.

"It had a real impact on me," he says. "I mean we stayed in this little cabin that was used later for life vests and canoe oars. I remember the impact of having this college-age guy as our counselor, a guy who was fun and talking to me about Jesus … and it was just so much cooler than what I was experiencing in my home church."

Jumping ahead nine years, when Brian was a college freshman at Western Michigan, he struggled with who he was. He struggled to maintain any relationship at all with God, drifting back and forth in the party scene. As he says, he was really kind of a mess. But on the very last day of his freshman year, his mother picked him up from college to take him home for the summer.

Before leaving, Brian wanted to quickly stop at the job fair hosted by the university. He felt completely overwhelmed when he walked in, staring down an aisle of nearly 400 booths. But right on the corner he spotted a SpringHill booth. Now he hadn't thought about the camp for nine years because he was never able to go back for financial reasons. And over the years, he had got into athletics, so SpringHill wasn't something he necessarily wanted to make time for.

Yet he snagged an application, went back home—and proceeded to work on a landscape crew for six weeks. Call it divine intervention, but Brian's allergies would not let up. So he pulled out the application two weeks before the camp was to open for the summer and saw that SpringHill needed a basketball coach.

He threw his hat in the ring and, before long, was called in for an interview by a veteran of SpringHill, R. O. Smith. His recollection of that interview is as follows:

> I blew the interview. I mean it was *bad*. The truth is I'd been in the bar the week before. I was a complete fraud at that point in my life, and he could smell it. The best part was when he asked me, "What's your favorite Bible story?" And I said, "'David and the Lion's Den.'" He stopped me and goes, "You mean Daniel?" Now I grew up in the church, but I was there every Sunday in defiance, not because I wanted to go. But I quickly caught myself and tried to recover by saying, "Oh yeah, that's what I meant. Actually, I love Gideon." And, somehow, I randomly remembered the story about Gideon. We laughed years later about that interview. R. O. said, "I knew you were full of it. I knew we were taking a risk, but every time I prayed about it, I felt like God was saying, 'Take a chance on this kid.'"

Brian got to SpringHill to take on his new job as the summer basketball coach, just one of the 400 college students who had been hired. Immediately, he felt as if he didn't fit in.

"Number one, I had never been around Christians that I thought were cool. So I was looking around and thinking, *These are actually people I'll hang out with. These people seem normal. They're athletic and they're creative and they just seem—normal.*"

But there was another reason Brian didn't feel he fit in with the others. He was living a double life. In those first four days of training, he packed up his car to leave *seven* times. And then, on the very last night of training, Mark Olson got up to speak. He delivered a powerful message about taking up your own personal cross and following Jesus.

"All I can tell you is the Holy Spirit did something in that moment that forever changed my life. Because I surrendered. I tell people all the time I was kind of holding one hand tight and the other open. And after that message, I opened both hands and let go, fully surrendering to Jesus. My life has never been the same since. That summer at SpringHill was when I shifted from thinking about my connection with God from a religion to a *relationship.*"

"The people were so pumped and excited to learn about Jesus. Counselors were always there for you, and campers became new-found family. However, the best part was completing activities that helped me conquer my fear of heights, then taking those activities and making them a learning experience for God." —Jillian

---

In the weeks that followed Brian's epiphany, someone handed him a book titled *Experiencing God.* He went through that workbook all summer and clearly remembers the experience:

> Ironically, I was a church kid who knew almost nothing about my faith. I didn't know where anything in the Bible was. I knew where Genesis, Matthew, and Revelation were, but beyond that I was lost. I didn't even know how to pray. I mean, literally, here was a kid who spent hours and hours and hours in the church, who knew virtually nothing. I remember sitting around campfires, during training, in a group of thirty, and memorizing parts of three or four different prayers as we went around the circle. And that is what I would use as my prayer because I didn't know how to pray, and I was too ashamed to tell them.

But what Brian didn't realize at the time was that the children in his charge didn't care about his prayers. They cared about his heart. All they saw was a young man who cared about them, who cared about Jesus. They didn't need him to have every answer and know where everything was in the Bible.

So he went back to college and, by winter time, was hired to be an area director at SpringHill. That second summer was good for Brian. He was definitely ready as a leader but still pretty immature. One day, he started a food fight in the cafeteria that got so out of control it was ridiculous.

"I remember sitting across from R. O. Smith. He was just shaking his head, like if he could have killed me, he would have. We had just destroyed the cafeteria and I felt horrible, because I was the one in charge. But he had grace for me."

Camp fires are another big memory for Brian. "Every week it

was a different group of SpringHill campers, and I always saw God move in a different way with each group. That was always exciting for me, to see what God would do with a group of kids, to see that moment. I was committed to wanting each kid to have such a great time and see you could actually have fun as a Christian."

There was one campfire memory Brian likely wants to forget. One night, he filled a pickup truck full of wood and built a bonfire that was so large that the top flame was over fifteen feet high. It got so hot that all the guys had to remove their shirts and back up so far that they were in a circle sixty feet from the other side. Brian remembers this moment fondly:

> It was so wide you couldn't even hear anything, and I did that on the night we were supposed to be sharing the Gospel. Here I was, the leader, trying to share about Jesus, and I created every reason in the world for the kids to be distracted. Yet I think those are the things that made my time at SpringHill what it was. I remember thinking then, *Man, someday, I want my kids to come to this place.*

Needless to say, years later, Brian's kids did attend a SpringHill day camp and overnight camp, and his whole family even went to our family camp.

It seems even when we are lost, God finds us and brings us home.

Today Brian is the founder of Overflow Church, a multicultural ministry in Benton Harbor, Michigan, that is celebrating ten years at the time of this publication. It started humbly with six people but has grown to well over three hundred. He's also the founder of Mosaic Christian

It seems even when we are lost, God finds us and brings us home.

Community Development, which runs four social enterprises. They have two restaurants, a resale store, and a lawn care company. Mosaic offers job training and employment for its community, which has a $17,000 median income and is 90 percent African American.

With his own ministry, Brian now speaks publically, fifty-two weeks of the year, or more often. His congregation would hardly believe that he was scared to death to speak in public prior to SpringHill:

> I [Brian] remember them thrusting a mic into my hand, having me interview a kid on stage for the final rally. I was so scared. I remember praying. There I was, a nineteen-year-old, and I'm interviewing this kid. That moment really set me up in so many ways, because SpringHill believed in me when I didn't believe in me.

> Some of the things we did on the weekend, just having those interactions and experiences—those were really big for me. The other thing was SpringHill's investment in leadership development. I had been captain of all my athletic teams. I played football, basketball, and baseball. I was actually the captain on all three. I was a natural-born leader. But I had never really been taught leadership. In fact, the coaches I had, unfortunately, rotated a lot. I can really say the first time I felt like I really began to be invested in, as a leader, was at SpringHill. There was a lot of good that came out of that place, experiences that made me think I could do anything.

Dave Bond also understands having life-altering experiences and creating lasting relationships at SpringHill all too well. After all, he met his wife there.

His SpringHill history goes back to the seventh grade, when we used to have something called Teen Week. Now, this was when the camp was much smaller, so Teen Week was seven days of camp that was exactly what it implied: for teenagers. Until then the camp had been mostly for younger kids. Then Teen Week came along, and we opened the camp exclusively to teens in an effort to connect with an older demographic. It was a mixture of boys and girls, and they did all kinds of crazy activities and had all kinds of fun competitions. Dave describes it as follows:

> I just remember it being one of the most amazing summers of my life. As I look back, there was certainly a very strong spiritual message in everything, and I was already a believer in Christ, but it definitely solidified my faith and encouraged me to see that there were a lot of other kids my age, teenagers, that could have faith in Christ, but still have a lot of fun and be crazy. A relationship with God didn't just have to be about going to church on Sundays. So it kind of opened up my eyes to what it meant to live out your faith in a different way.

And then, as the years went by, Dave got involved in his local church along with various youth groups, and he forgot all about SpringHill—that is, until he went away to Michigan State:

> I just was getting done with my freshman year in college. I went to one of those summer job fairs and, lo and behold, one of the tables was a camp called SpringHill. There was a guy sitting behind the table, and as I started looking at the information, it suddenly dawned on me that I'd been there before. So I took the application, asked some questions, and applied. Eventually I got a job there, and I ended up working at SpringHill as a counselor that first year.

Back in those days, camp was six days a week, so you literally had less than a twenty-four-hour break before the next group of campers came in. And so most of my first two years was spent with campers. When you're the first-year counselor, you spend an awful lot of time with the youngest kids, which means you're in Teepee Village. I have nothing but fond memories there. I also have nothing but memories of feeling absolutely exhausted all the time because you literally only had a one-hour break back in those days. Once you had your hour break, you were right back at it with the kids. But I do remember at one point walking by what was then the swimming hole; now it's just a little pond. We didn't have a pool back then. I remember walking. I was coming off one of my breaks and just kind of praising God and singing, and I remember thinking to myself for the first time in my life that I felt like I was at a place where I didn't wish I was somebody else. I didn't wish I was somewhere else. It was like I suddenly realized and said to myself, "I feel sorry for everybody else in the world who isn't here right now."

As hard as it was to spend almost twenty-four hours with six- and seven-year-olds, Dave says it was still the most satisfying spiritual time of his life. In years two and three, he started to do what was called area directing. We were just starting our Teen Service Team program at the time, kind of shaping it and figuring out what it even looked like. Dave remembers this time as follows:

That was a lot of fun because for the first two years I was obviously talking to and leading young kids, but by that third summer I was talking to and leading young adults. Whether they were other counselors or teenagers who were trying to figure out life, we'd do these talks at the campfires, or morning Bible studies. And for me that was critical because it totally framed my lack of fear of speaking in front of people. It took away any fear of public speaking. It took away any fear of the unknown questions, and being able to be flexible on the spot. And so it kind of made me realize I was good in front of people. I loved to teach, I loved to talk. And although I didn't realize it at the time, it was shaping me into the type of person that would feel comfortable teaching, talking, and counseling.

It had such a great impact on my life that I came back again the second year and counseled again. And then that led that into my third year, when I became an area director. That third summer, I really thought I was done. But God obviously had other plans. I thought I was going to graduate from college and just go out and get a job like everybody else, but it ended up that I couldn't get licensed that summer for the job I had interviewed for to become a financial advisor and get into the investment business. There were some studies and other things that had to be done first, so I decided, what the heck, I'll go back to camp one more time. I'm glad I did. Not only because of the experience but because that's the summer I met the woman who would become my wife. Thirty years later, Phyllis and I are still happily married.

I had actually met her very briefly at Michigan State, but our connection was SpringHill. Mutual friends knew that she was going to work there that summer and they told her that she should talk to me, so we made a connection once I started working there.

Dave explains how SpringHill was very instrumental, not only in his relationships and connections, but also spiritually:

I'd say the thing that really impacted me the most spiritually happened just after my freshman year in college. I went away to Michigan State, and I was trying to go to church on Sunday mornings. I really felt at the time like I was the only Christian on campus, even though I know that wasn't true. I just never really found a place to get connected there, and so when I worked that summer at SpringHill, even though I had been a believer my whole life, it just completely transformed my motivation, my outlook, just everything about what it meant to be a Christian as far as my focus. I made a commitment to turn my life over fully to Christ that summer, and I decided when I got back to campus I was really going to seek out a group of people that were trying to serve the Lord. So, I did. When I got back to Michigan State, I found Campus Crusade for Christ and got involved there on campus. I have to say that SpringHill was the catalyst, and has been really the foundation and the seed that planted a whole lot of things in my life.

While at Michigan State I was a communication major. I went there originally to be a broadcaster and either get into being a DJ or to do something with TV or radio. But eventually, I started taking business classes, as well as more counseling classes. In fact, for a while there I thought I'd go on to seminary and maybe become a youth pastor. But when I got out of college, I needed to get a job. My dad had put me through school, and he couldn't afford to also put me through grad school or seminary.

So I took a job in the financial service industry. And then something remarkable happened. I was maybe a year into that job, thinking that I was just going to make some money and then move on to something I was more passionate about, but then I started realizing I was counseling people on their finances, helping them plan for the future, and talking to them about some of the most important things of their lives, either family, finances, or what they believed, their faith. So I began to think of life as a three-legged stool—family, finances, and faith—really the three pivotal areas in a person's life. And I was having the privilege of being able to help people in all three of those areas with my career.

I look back and SpringHill is the one thing that really honed every one of those skills: family, finances, and faith. I was able to really put everything in perspective. I mean you didn't make a lot of money working at camp, but you also realized that it wasn't always about the money. So, when I look back, I could not have had a better training for what I was going to go into for the rest of my career. And thirty-two years later I'm still going strong.

In time, my wife and I had kids of our own, three of them. I was so anxious and excited when they got old enough to go to SpringHill. We would go up there for family camps, just introduce them to the environment. I remember when my son, Trevor, first went there when he was six, right after first grade. Even though we loved the camp, Phyllis and I, we dropped them off at what is called The Fort. You could usually hop on a bus or a wagon to take you back to the parking lot from there, but I just remember we were crying so much that we decided we'd walk because even though we knew it was a great place and a safe place, it was our first kid being dropped off at camp. And with that came the amazing feeling of knowing what a great experience it was going to be for him.

Every one of our kids has a strong faith and most of them—I actually think all of them—would credit SpringHill for much of what they believe and why they believe it. So, yeah, it had a huge impact. For me, it's been a full-circle kind of experience. I knew everybody there and got to know, back in the day, Enoch Olson and Mark Olson. Mark was, actually, a good friend, and I was tremendously sad when he passed away. That was rough. I had known Michael Perry, and when he took over at SpringHill, of course I naturally carried a little bit of trepidation because I knew Mark so well. But I have to say that Michael just picked up the torch where Mark left it and he kept on marching. A few years later, through my contact with them, Michael reached out to me and asked if I'd be on the board. So, now I've really had a full-circle experience from camper to staff to camper-parent to finally being on the board.

It has all been such a great pleasure to serve.

From served to serving, God's plan will always bring us full-circle.

That reflects our God-immersed

From served to serving, God's plan will always bring us full-circle.

idea: we create an experience The SpringHill Way, but we really do trust that God's going to do what he's going to do in kids' lives, and in our staff's lives. We don't try to force it. We just know if we create experiences The SpringHill Way, God does show up.

"Camp will make history in your life. You have fun, but at the same time you learn about God. Last year, after I left camp, I got really into reading the Bible and it changed my relationship with God. I learned that God works in many different ways and He will always forgive everybody no matter how they sin." —Heidi

---

Kids say all the time that this is the place where they feel God shows up in their lives. I believe it.

Reflection on Journeys of Faith and Friendship

Over the past couple of years or so, I've attempted through trial and error to improve my photography. I used a Canon Rebel, mostly on auto focus because I didn't know a thing about the camera and very little about shooting a quality photograph.

I'd read the camera's manual as well as a photography book in an attempt to improve. As a result, I knew just enough to be dangerous, but not enough to be better. What's worse, the reading and practice gave me a false sense of confidence in what I thought I knew and could do. So, in hopes of making some improvement, I decided to sit in on a training session for our summer photographers and videographers, facilitated by Chris duMond from our marketing and design firm, DesignVox.

The key learning element required us to shoot photos of people at camp, picking our best ones and sharing them with the group. The group then critiqued our photos by having all the group members mention something they liked and something to improve.

As the team reviewed my photo, I realized that *critique* was the missing piece in my attempts to become a better photographer. If I were going to improve, I needed input and perspective from others, especially those experienced in photography.

As you reflect on the most powerful moments in your life, what role did others play in those moments? Do you have a small community of like-minded people encouraging each other to make hopes and dreams a reality? Do you encourage the children in your life to engage in their community? How does God use other community members to play a role in your life?

CHAPTER FIVE

All Kids Are Special

"Like Jesus we accept children as they are, not because of their appearance, their athletic ability, not because of their academic ability or how talented they are, but because they are created in the image of God." —Mark Olson

---

Including *All* God's Children

- If you don't have a child with special needs, you may not be aware of the rejection and apathy they face. For parents and caregivers, this is especially painful.

- Children are particularly open with their hearts and acceptance. Do you think this is inherent or taught?

- Those who have spent time with children who have special needs often remark that the relationship is a dual blessing. Have you ever thought about how this fits into God's plan?

It was a hot Indiana summer when I paid a visit to our overnight camp tucked in the southern part of the state. I sat in the dining hall as the meal was wrapping up. The campers filed out, and the high-school crew, the TSTers, were doing their work, clearing off the tables and cleaning up the dining area. And I noticed this young man, who happened to be in a wheelchair, just scooting around. It was electric so he could power it easily, and he was going around from table to table while the other TSTers were loading his lap with dirty dishes. When he had all he could handle, he would drive them over to the dish room.

I just watched all of them do this, and he was having an absolute blast. So I went up to him, introduced myself, and learned his name was Marcus. I thanked him for what he was doing, and he beamed and said he was having a great time. He just loved being a part of the team, serving, and making a difference.

Later that summer, I was back at our camp in Indiana, in the dining hall, almost the exact same setting, and curiously, I saw Marcus again, cruising around doing the same job he had been doing earlier in the summer. Now, our experiences are a two-week program, so he shouldn't have been there. But he was back.

I walked up to him. "Marcus, I see you're back. Why are you here, doing this all over again?"

"Mr. Perry," he said, "when I'm at SpringHill, it's the only time I feel like a normal kid."

That is part of The SpringHill Experience, embracing all kids, taking them for who they are and how they're created, *including* them. We don't segregate those with disabilities or special needs into subgroups. We include them in the community, and Marcus felt a part of this small community of campers and staff. The fact he was in a wheelchair wasn't a hindrance; it was a benefit. He took advantage of it, and he just loved being part of a team.

Marcus did that for a couple of seasons, and when he graduated from high school he decided he wanted to work for us all summer. So we hired him as our front desk receptionist and phone operator at our camp in Indiana. I remember, during staff training that first year, he worked full-time; we were all in a large group for the kick-off training.

"Your buddy Marcus is here," I began. "He's going to be on the team this year. But here's the deal. The only way Marcus can really be effective and be on this team is if we have some guys who are committed to help him get dressed every morning, get in his wheelchair, get to his post at the phone, and make sure he can do all he needs to do."

A half dozen guys raised their hands. "Hey, we got this. We'll be with him all summer. We'll make sure it all happens."

So every year, our summer staff rallied around him and helped him, and he was an integral part of the team for the three summers he worked for us.

Every single one of us has a purpose, and every single one of us belongs.

That's the essence of our philosophy. We'll do whatever it takes to include every child. We've had deaf, blind, and fully wheelchair-bound children, and we feed

Every single one of us has a purpose, and every single one of us belongs.

them, we dress them, we make sure to do anything and everything necessary so they get the full experience. If we can and we have the staff available, we'll even give them one-on-one attention. We have nursing and medical staff on hand to address all their needs. And as with all our kids, our staff members are all fully trained to make sure that all dietary and physical needs are met. Here's one parent's experience with sending her autistic son to SpringHill:

> After seeing the camp in action on a video at a SpringHill day camp, my boys really wanted to go. It was a go from

the start for my two youngest, but I wasn't sure about our oldest, Parker, who has autism. I called the camp with my questions and was elated to find out that they had a one-on-one program that he qualified for. I immediately signed him up. He had such a wonderful experience with Joe his first year. I remember seeing Parker with Joe from a distance—not hard; Joe is really tall and Parker was on his shoulders at the big celebration on the last day. It was tear jerking to see Parker snuggle into Joe's side in a great big hug. Parker did *not* want to come home that day. He told me, this year, he wants to go for all summer! SpringHill is a wonderful experience for *all* of God's children! Thank you so much. I never worry when my kids are at SpringHill, hours away from home.

To make sure they're included, if we have campers in a wheelchair, for example, and they can't move, we will literally carry them up to the top of the zipline. We'll put them in the harness and we'll send them down with the rest of their cabin mates. I see this almost weekly at SpringHill, where a leader is on the climbing wall, carrying a camper up to the top so that he or she can ring the bell. There is just no accommodation too great to make.

That's the idea of community, the idea of embracing *all* kids. Marcus reflected the joy that comes with being part of our community. That's one of my favorite mental pictures when I think of SpringHill: Marcus growing up through SpringHill, serving, giving back, and being embraced by the community. And in that embrace, he understood the love of Christ because of what he experienced in that community, and what he learned in serving.

And from the beginning, SpringHill has welcomed and embraced children with special needs. When Enoch Olson's son took over the camp in the early 1980s, children with special needs took on a very personal note: he and his wife, Lisa (who was also on staff), were the parents of an autistic child, which made them all the more aware and capable of responding to children with special needs, many of whom are paired with one specially trained counselor, reflecting SpringHill's longstanding belief that every child is created uniquely in the image and likeness of God.

The Power of Inclusion

Josh Maycoff exemplifies The SpringHill Way and our camps' inclusion program. He became accustomed to rejection early in life. He struggled with difficulties in communicating, similar to Asperger's syndrome, and he had ADHD and real trouble fitting in and getting along with others. When he became frustrated over his inability to complete a task, he acted out, so much so that it proved too much for day-care centers and organized sports teams. Josh's mother, Karen, constantly received calls from these facilities explaining that Josh couldn't return because they couldn't handle him effectively or respond adequately to his needs.

After a few years of day camp, she decided to enroll Josh in a SpringHill overnight camp. Not surprisingly, she had more than a little bit of ambivalence: while she was overjoyed to be able to send Josh to SpringHill, she still wondered if her son would be able to do it.

Dan, Josh's counselor, who was specifically trained to work with special-needs kids, ensured Josh felt welcomed from the moment he arrived at camp: "We just need to make them feel like kids, and that's a rarity for a lot of special-needs children," Dan assured Karen. "In the end, they're just like every other kid. They just want to have fun and know they are all children of God. Kids at SpringHill always embrace children with special needs. It's awesome to see other kids in the cabin come around children with special needs and show them love, their love, God's love."

Josh squealed with delight when he fired a slingshot and hit his target: a tree. "Awesome!" other campers shouted.

When Josh strapped on a harness to speed down the zipline, everybody yelled encouraging words, teaching him by example. The counselors put him in charge of the zipline. The boy beamed with newfound pride and savored being accepted and embraced instead of rejected as he was elsewhere.

That, his mom said, made all the difference: "Josh went to camp that year and had a one-to-one counselor, and he loved it. He had such a good time he couldn't wait to go back. This year will be his fourth year at an overnight camp and his sister's second year. I have even been up to camp for the women's retreat and to volunteer. We love SpringHill. It has become part of our family. It's great that they included him in everything. So often, he has been separated out or thrown out of day cares."

Josh paused at the shoreline as other kids plunged into the lake, but with a bit of encouragement, soon raced into the water.

By the lake, in a quiet one-on-one conversation, Dan found a teachable moment, and said softly to Josh, "Do you think Moses trusted that God was going to help him out?"

"Yes," Josh replied, "because God never breaks a promise."

Josh thrived. His mom had grown accustomed to warning him to slow down, take it easy. SpringHill counselors showed her a more positive, life-affirming, loving response. At Family Day, she marveled as the counselors told him not to make fun of other campers but to encourage them.

SpringHill provides the environment and experiences to ensure all kids learn and thrive.

Last summer, I talked to three or four parents a week who had checked the box on our parent survey indicating that they'd be willing to talk to somebody from SpringHill in a ten-minute phone call. On one of those calls, I talked to a dad from

SpringHill provides the environment and experiences to ensure all kids learn and thrive.

Chicago. He was … well, I don't even know if he was a man of faith. We never got that far. He was very businesslike. I don't know if he was an attorney, or investment banker, or what, but he gave me eight minutes exactly. So I asked him what the experience was like, and he went on to tell me how he had found out about SpringHill's inclusion program from someone he'd met at a movie. His son had Down syndrome, so he brought him to SpringHill from Chicago, never knowing anything other than this random recommendation.

"When we picked him up," he said, "we thought our son was a rock star. Everybody knew him. Counselors, kids, they were all high-fiving. They loved him. He was like the camp rock star."

"Our son, Isaac, has autism and has been to respite overnight but never to an overnight camp. When we arrived at SpringHill, one of the summer staff members had actually worked with Isaac previously, at Smith Respite. Her excitement to see Isaac made me feel very secure in leaving him. They got along great. He loves playing in the water and swimming, and she was a lifeguard! I really appreciated the quality of care my special-needs son received and how much fun he had. Good job SpringHill!" —SpringHill Parent

---

That's what it's like for a camper with special needs at SpringHill: rock star status, that warm embrace. What we've learned, even though it can be difficult, is that kind of diversity and that kind of inclusion blesses and benefits the *entire* community. Just ask Kelly Korbel:

My name is Kelly Korbel and I went to SpringHill three times while I was growing up, probably around 1998 or so. I am e-mailing because I have thought about something today that I haven't thought about in years and wanted to reach out to express my gratitude.

It didn't seem like a big deal to my eight-year-old self that my older brother, Patrick, was coming to summer camp with me one year. It seemed like the natural thing to do, and I couldn't understand why it hadn't happened before. You see, my brother is severely disabled and requires full care. As a child, I didn't see that this would be a very difficult situation to accommodate at a summer camp filled with physical activities, but thinking back now, I want to let you know how grateful I am that Patrick could go to summer camp that year. The only thing I remember SpringHill accommodating for was his age (he was too old to go to camp), but I now see the efforts that must have been involved in his stay. Feeding and pushing a wheelchair through the woods alone are a lot to ask, not to mention bathing, diapering, and changing.

From a child's perspective, I didn't notice anything different about my brother's stay at SpringHill than my own. He wore a life jacket and someone held him so he could experience the thrill of the blob. He went tandem ziplining. He ate in the cafeteria. He went to all of the campfires, all of the prayer groups, down the water slides, and pretty much everything else that all campers got to do.

I remember there was a mural being painted while we were at camp, and I'm curious if it is still there or if it has been painted over. Patrick was in that mural, being pushed in his wheelchair by a counselor. Please know that it was this mural that made me think of SpringHill today and prompted me to reach out to you to say thank you. Thank you for taking such good care of Patrick, and thank you for everything that you do every day to touch the lives of kids like us. SpringHill holds some of my best memories.

The Influence of Our Inclusion Program

Our blessings with our inclusion program have amazing origins. Many years ago, a couple from Pella, Iowa, named Arvin and Darlene Van Hall, were in Michigan at their son's house, helping him do some work, getting the house settled and having new appliances installed. They had ordered the appliances from a local furniture store, which happened to be owned by people who were really involved with SpringHill.

The person installing the appliances, Joe, happened to work for us. He had a young family and was doing some side work installing appliances to make some extra money for a house. It was a Saturday, and it turned out Joe was missing a part to finish the installation. He told the Van Halls he would come back, but he couldn't come back until Monday because he had to work at his other job.

"What's your other job?" Arvin asked.

"I work for a Christian camp called SpringHill. Tomorrow's our opening day."

The Van Halls had been involved with a little Christian camp back in Pella, so their interest was piqued.

"Any chance we could come visit? We'd love to do a tour."

"I used to be shy, doubt myself all the time, and have no confidence in myself. After coming here, God showed me how wonderful I am and I have come to better terms with my disability. I realize that it is a gift now, and it's amazing when I see that I can use my disability to impact people … SpringHill has meant so much to me and has completely changed my life. God works in this place and you just feel Him all around." —Melody

---

So Joe called me and we set it up. The Van Halls were blown away. They had never seen anything like SpringHill; it was way more than what they were working with at the camp in Iowa.

Being a very sharp, self-made man, Arvin started asking me all kinds of questions about how we operated camp, the financial situation, and how it all worked.

When we were finished, he said, "We're working with this camp in Iowa that's just trying to start up. We have a piece of property that we talked about giving them so they could build a camp, but I don't have a lot of confidence they have a plan that will work. I'm hesitant to give them this property until I know they have a really good solid plan. Would you or SpringHill be willing to take a look at what they're doing, and maybe, there's a partnership between SpringHill and this other camp?"

Arvin and Darlene love kids, so I think they really wanted to do something for kids in Iowa, and they loved the idea of camp. Arvin's a big outdoorsman: hunting, fishing, and farming. We've always had this really openhanded thing about SpringHill. We'll help other like-minded organizations any way we can. So he invited me out, and we went to Iowa. I brought a couple of our other team members and went to their board meeting. We saw the property. Then we came back and met with churches, talked about it, and made an assessment. Did we want to partner with them? What would that even look like?

At the time, our day camps were taking off. We didn't need another overnight camp in Iowa. It just didn't make sense for us. So after about a year of talking, assessing, meeting with their staff, and board, we said no.

But Arvin was persistent. He came back to me and said, "How about this? Would you be open if we paid you to come out and meet with the staff and work with this camp, and evaluate it?" Arvin is a pretty straight shooter. "Part of what I really would love for you to do is just help me understand if they are really capable of pulling this off? What's your assessment of it? Can you help them?"

So he and Darlene sent us a $5,000 check and said they had covered the costs of my travel and time, and whatever was left over was to go to scholarships. Well, I went out there. I met with everybody. The next year they wanted me to come back, so they sent us $10,000. I did it again. The third year, another $10,000. I was beginning to really appreciate and love Arvin and Darlene.

Each year, I went out there, and each year, they kept giving us money, more money to go in the scholarship fund. Finally, I went out and we followed the same routine, but I decided I needed to share with them what we were doing at SpringHill. They had clearly become donors to SpringHill because of the amount of money they kept giving us each year.

We went to breakfast one morning, in this little café in Pella, Iowa.

"Look," I said. "I don't want to take a single penny away from this other camp, but I feel like I owe it to you to let you know what's going on because you've been giving money to SpringHill now for a while. You've been covering my costs to come out here, but there's been more than enough, and we've been able to scholarship kids."

We had a booklet that talked about all the things we were working on and raising money for, so I flipped through the book with Arvin, and we got to a page with a photo that's now famous at SpringHill. At the time, I wasn't really paying attention, but both Arvin and Darlene stopped on this page, and I couldn't get them to move past it. I wanted to get them to the end of the book, where we talk about how much money we're trying to raise and how we're doing.

Arvin got up abruptly. "You've got to excuse me. I need to go to the bathroom." And he walked away.

I sat there with Darlene, talking a little bit and thinking, *This isn't going well.* I had no idea what was going on. Arvin, eventually, came back and sat down.

"Can ... we finish going through the book?" I asked awkwardly. "Are you okay going through the rest?"

"Sure," he said, and we went through the book.

That was it. After breakfast I said to Arvin, "I've never seen your plant. I would love to see it."

We drove through Pella, and on part of the trip to their plant, we drove through a golf course that he owned with a couple other people and that was costing him a whole bunch of money. As a matter of fact, they were selling it, and he would have to put money with it to get it sold.

I had heard about this, so I said, "I'm really sorry we have to drive through this golf course … and remind you of all this."

And he said to me, "Michael, what really makes me mad is that money. I could've given it to you so you could build some special-needs housing for that kid in that wheelchair."

Huh? What kid? I thought.

"In that picture in your book," he said, and I remembered which picture it was: a camper with his counselor. The camper's in a wheel chair, and they're playing crud wars, which is a tradition for middle-schoolers. Two teams throw flour, water, and oats, and, well, it's just a giant, food fight mess. The camper in his wheelchair and his counselor are in the middle of it. Flour is flying everywhere, and the camper's got this huge grin on his face. One of our summer leaders took the photograph. (We hire summer interns to do all our photography, so most of the photography in our marketing materials has been done by college students.)

"Why don't we pray that something works out, and you can do that," I said, and that was the end of it.

Or so I thought.

The next day, I flew home, landed in Grand Rapids, and was driving up to Camp Michigan when I received a call from Arvin.

"Hey, I want to call you and just let you know that Darlene and I didn't sleep a wink last night. We couldn't get that camper, that kid's face, out of our mind all night, and here's what we want to do. We want to build that special-needs housing." That was one of the projects in the back of the book, probably about $350,000. "We want to build that, and we want to do it in honor of that camper. We want to honor him, and we want to know who he is, what his story is, what his history is, and we want to connect with him."

Well, I knew the photo, and I looked at it often, but I had no idea who the camper was. I'd seen him, but I'd never met him. So, I got back to camp and went to our marketing and development people.

"Who is this kid?"

Thankfully, our program people knew. "Oh, his name's Colin Northrup. He has cerebral palsy."

Before long I was on the phone with Colin's mom, Dawn. She had seen the photo, and so I went on to tell her the story of what had happened.

She was crying as she spoke. "You need to know that this is the story of Colin's life. This kid, who's never supposed to be able to talk or communicate, God gave him the ability to speak, and he can talk, even though he has cerebral palsy."

She said that his whole life has always been about giving voice to those who don't have a voice. I told her his photo gave voice to all those kids and moved the Van Halls to give us money.

Eventually, we introduced them, and there's a big connection now between Colin and the Van Halls, and I get to know the Northrups. Now that they know who he is, they want to honor Colin, somehow, with the building. Well, we don't name buildings after people at SpringHill. We've never done that. We'll thank people in a plaque for their contribution, a number of people, but we're not into building naming. The building was going to be in a village of cabins, all named after 14,000-foot peaks in the United States, such as Mt. Hood and Pike's Peak. So we're building this cabin, and the theme of the village is peaks, and yet this donor wants to do this honoring. Arvin didn't exactly say to name the building, but he and Darlene wanted to honor Colin somehow.

By this point, our marketing team was fully engaged. One of them did a little research and found out that in the Canadian Rockies, there's a 14,000-foot peak called ... Colin Ridge.

God's intricate design is to connect us all in his grace.

Since then, the Van Halls have been fully involved with us, including building two bathhouses down in Indiana and

God's intricate design is to connect us all in his grace.

rebuilding our teepees in Michigan. And now they're in the process of building another housing village down in Indiana. They've also given us money to fund scholarships for special-needs kids such as Colin.

"At the beginning of the week I realized we had a camper with special needs in our cabin. At first I turned away from him, not thinking about his feelings like I should have been. After a day or two I grew closer to God through prayer and reading the Bible. That was when I finally realized that the camper I had turned away from was really the best part about our cabin. Being able to see him have fun and grow with God really helped me become closer to God. Because of that camper and this experience I got to witness the full power of the Lord." —Tyler

---

The SpringHill Way is to embrace all kids. Embracing them means welcoming them, bringing them in, and fully including them in the camp program as much as humanly possible. It really is about this idea of embracing, as we did with Marcus and Colin. They participate in all activities and they live in the cabins if they're able to. We don't put kids in an environment they can't manage. That's why we have Colin's Ridge, which offers housing for kids who need a little extra. We do everything we can to integrate them into normal camp life.

We bring them all together. We're not going to be segregated. The beauty is, to be honest with you, that kids understand diversity and inclusivity way better than adults do.

Kids embrace and welcome diversity and inclusivity.

Reflections on All Kids Are Special

"I just want to say thank you. SpringHill has just been fantastic for my son. I only wish the rest of the world could be more like SpringHill."

These words were addressed to me and a small group of our year-round staff during the closing day of camp by a father of a camper with special needs. The father went on to explain that his son had been coming to SpringHill for a number of summers and it was always the highlight of his son's year. It was the week when his son felt accepted and loved as a "normal" kid.

I believe it's this acceptance and love that the dad was referring to when he said, almost to himself, "I only wish the rest of the world could be more like SpringHill."

Of course, it's always great to hear this kind of unsolicited feedback from a parent. Our goal is that every kid will feel as this camper did and experience the love of Christ through our staff and in the small communities we create.

This father's wish has had me thinking. I've realized his wish really isn't a wish at all, but our ultimate mission.

SpringHill exists to create experiences where Christ can transform the lives of young people. These experiences include embracing all kinds of kids, regardless of who they are, what they've done, or where they've come from. Yet, as powerful as this is, The SpringHill Experience isn't an end unto itself; it's part of something bigger.

That something bigger is the Church's work of bringing the values and reality of Christ's Kingdom into the world. In other words, we haven't thoroughly done our job unless our campers and staff are leaving SpringHill and bringing a little of it back into the world, making the world a little more like SpringHill, which really means making the world little more like Christ's Kingdom.

What do you do to make the world a little more like Christ's Kingdom? What does it mean that a child is created in the image of God? How does that affect how we love that child? Are there people or children in your life who are on the fringes of their community, those who need to know they're special in God's eyes? What does your community do for them? What can *you* do for them? What kind of impact does including these people in a community have on others in that community?

CHAPTER SIX

A Summer of Giving Lasts a Lifetime

"Whatever you do, work heartily, as for the Lord and not men, know that from the Lord you will receive the inheritance as your reward. You are serving the Lord Jesus Christ." —Colossians 3:23–24

Finding Your Purpose

- Every one of us is here for a reason. God gave each one of us a specific purpose.

- If we believe that everyone has a purpose, that means that we do too. Are you on the path you believe you were meant to be on? What steps can you take to figure out what God intended for you to do?

- What events in your youth shaped what you believe your purpose to be? Have you strayed from your purpose at one time or another? Why?

I was with my wife, driving from Indianapolis to Grand Rapids, and kind of halfway between the cities there's a Starbucks. I felt I needed to perk up to make the rest of the drive home, so we pulled off the expressway and headed in to get some coffee. On the way to the counter, I spotted a group of twelve, or so, of our summer leaders.

Now, what's really funny is that along with a couple of groups from the two colleges located not far from that expressway exit was a group of summer leaders from the University of Michigan in Ann Arbor, a good three hours away. Apparently, they had come down for the weekend to spend some time with their coworkers and study together. I thought, *How great is that—that they continue those kinds of relationships and maintain those meaningful connections outside SpringHill?*

But that's the thing with our counselors, our summer leaders. When they leave SpringHill, whether it's for the fall or for the rest of their lives, they understand that even though they may have had this close group of friends that they connected with while at work, this faith group, they're part of a larger community.

This is especially true for our college-age staff, who are in the thick of education and thinking about their future, their direction in life. I'd say the two things that have come out of college students who have worked for SpringHill are a sense of direction and, though it sounds funny, the propensity for those young people to end up meeting their future spouse. I suppose it's like that with other professions, but it's not only about the work-related interests they have in common. The couples who form that kind of bond also have similar motivations and goals. And they get to see in their partners innate qualities of compassion, genuine kindness, and empathy, in action.

SpringHill could not be what it is today without our summer leaders, who, in so many ways, become the face of the camp experience for our kids. To restate one of the key elements of SpringHill success: campers get the same counselor throughout the week, and the counselors stay in the same cabin with their charges throughout the camp. This allows the counselors to get to know the kids well and fosters close personal relationships grounded in faith. Counselors teach by their Christian example, by their questions, eliciting profound insights into what it means to live according to our Lord's teachings, by gently guiding them to discern the right path, and to choose it, with unshakable conviction.

Our counselor-centered model has achieved astounding success over the decades, beginning with the rigorous, independent, criminal, and sex-offender background checks of 2,500 candidates a year. The interviewing process determines where they are in their respective spiritual journeys, and how they would likely interact with children to bring the Gospels to life. The 1,000 "chosen ones" undergo intensive training, learning not only about how to interact with campers, always seeking and capitalizing on "teachable moments," but also critically important safety protocols, child protection, conflict management, and first-aid skills. Staff are trained to ensure the safety of children throughout their stays, freeing counselors to focus on directing activities, building strong, faith-based relationships along with memories and lessons that last a lifetime.

And in all this, the summer leaders inevitably get as much out of the camp as they give. As they teach, they learn, enriching and deepening not only the campers' personal relationship with Christ but also their own, while developing leadership and mentoring skills that help prepare them for fulfilling careers.

In fact, an independent survey of counselors, commissioned by SpringHill, found the overwhelming majority of them reported serving as a counselor strengthened their spiritual development, made them more open to sharing their faith with others, and transformed them into leaders. Counselors also said that they developed markedly as Christians in their work life and that the experience guided their career choices and helped them attain jobs.

And they have a blast along the way.

Jacob Kerr, a counselor at the 2016 overnight camp in Indiana and now a junior marketing major at Purdue University, said, "This summer job might be the most important summer of my life. We get to zipline, play paintball, ride horses, slide, run, dance, go crazy. Being a summer leader at SpringHill brings out the kid in me and has been an amazing break from the demands and distractions of life."

Tyler Gifford, a SpringHill counselor for three years, described how the experience blended fun and faith … and also challenges. He recalled dance parties breaking out spontaneously, gaga ball matches, and slip 'n' slide races. But he also remembers those quiet conservations about Jesus, and about the community:

> I have been privileged to witness the Body of Christ in action. I glimpsed community in the encouraging notes we wrote to each other. I felt community in the times of affirmation we intentionally set aside to exhort each other. I saw community in the tears shed together. I experienced community in the prayers we prayed over one another. I watched community on the days that we bore each other's burdens. I received community through the endless laughter and hilarious inside jokes.

SpringHill could not be what it is today without the strength of our summer leaders, and the lifelong lessons they both impart and take away from the experience of this unique Christian community.

And it's such a powerful experience for our summer leaders, because they really are leading, not chaperoning or babysitting.

Over and over again, they'll remark that what they learned through their training and the hands-on experience has had a real impact on their careers and their families, and how they lead and teach their own kids.

And I think our goal has been, from the broader community standpoint, to

SpringHill could not be what it is today without the strength of our summer leaders.

help our summer leaders see that it's really in the context of community that you can grow in your faith, experience faith, and do things together. You *can* make a difference in the world.

The Difference a Summer Can Make

Jessica Concannon proves that. She worked at SpringHill for five summers, her first being after her sophomore year of college. "The summer before, I had stayed at home and worked at the Gap, and at a neighbor's law firm. I was like, *This is the most miserable way to spend my summer. Surely there's something better I could be doing, making money but doing something more enjoyable.*"

That's when one of her friends from college, who had worked at SpringHill, told Jessica about the gymnastics program. Having been a gymnast her whole life and having coached as well, Jessica was more than intrigued by the opportunity. But by the time Jessica interviewed for the position, we had already discontinued our gymnastics program. Instead, she was offered a position as part of our TST program.

"I really hadn't worked with teenagers much," Jessica says. "I was grateful they were offering me a job, but that really wasn't what I thought I was gonna be doing. I was a little leery because I was only nineteen, so I was gonna be pretty close in age to most of my campers. But I decided to give it a try."

After a couple of days of staff training that first week, Jessica had found her passion. "You bond so deeply with the people that you're working with, and you share your faith stories and just stories about life, and I was like, *Wow. This is gonna be an amazing summer. I cannot believe I get to live and work with all these incredible people all summer.*"

But fairly quickly, Jessica realized that other teenagers were going through really difficult, challenging situations she hadn't gone through. Her parents divorced when she was younger, which certainly can be traumatic for all involved, but she was fortunate enough to not have had to go through even more traumatic experiences or struggles that the young people in her charge were going through.

"I remember my first group. I had them for three weeks. There were kids struggling with cutting, struggling with eating disorders, depression, and suicide, and my eyes were just really opened to what teenagers were going through and how much they needed Jesus. They needed hope."

"My counselors helped me realize that I am not alone in this world and that someone else is going through the same pain and loneliness that I feel sometimes." —Larica

---

She grew personally that summer, just learning how to deal with really hard, traumatic conversations. She remembers the nights going to bed, crying, hoping that her kids, her campers couldn't hear her, simply heartbroken over some of her kids' lives. Yet God used that opportunity to prepare her for what was to come.

SpringHill taught her how to be a leader. The first year she was a counselor, and then every year after that, she was an area director. She worked with teenagers all four years, and in her last year, she did day camp, traveling around western Michigan. As an area director, she oversaw a team of four counselors, as well as all the kids on the team. And she had to work with other area directors of other teams, as well as the leadership staff, overseeing everything. This gave her not only the experience of leading a large group of people but also of learning how to pour into them, spiritually, making sure their physical needs were met by getting breaks and helping them to navigate hard situations with other campers. Jessica remembers it as follows:

It was a lot of prayer and a lot of dependence on the Holy Spirit. And then, also learning how to go to people above me to ask for help. I think the most transformative memory I have was during my second summer there. Our Bible study for the summer really focused on justice, so we talked to our students a lot about what God's view of justice is, what it looks like to bring justice to the places where we live, and to the world. Prior to that, I had started spending a lot of time in Detroit doing photography, and I would just meet people on the streets and hear their stories and was really captivated by the potential of what God could do in the inner city. So then, over the summer, I met many like-minded people who had really huge hearts to bring justice to inner city areas, specifically through education, so it was actually at SpringHill where I got the vision for what I would eventually do with my life.

We were all educators, or going into education, and I remember so vividly the conversation. We were sitting around at the pond, me and two other friends, just talking about what we could do: "What can we do to bring justice to the education system and make things more equitable, especially Christian education?"

"I'm gonna start an inner city school," I replied, "an inner-city Christian school that anyone can afford. That's what I'm gonna do. This is what I feel God wants me to do."

Today Jessica is the founder and principal of an inner-city Christian school. Everything she experienced at SpringHill, the hard times with the teenagers, the leadership roles, prepared her for her purpose in life: to serve inner-city children. Jessica explains the mission of her organization as follows:

Our mission is to be a Christ-centered school that any family can afford. To accomplish that, we do charge tuition, but we charge families 5 percent of their income, and that is per family, not per child. So whether they have one or five children, it costs the same for their family. That's very challenging for us, of course. We do tons of fundraising, tons of networking, but what that does is connect people to our story, and what we're doing, and what God's doing in our community.

Aside from making a Christian education affordable and accessible to anybody who wants it, our main goals are to provide an option that didn't formerly exist and to make disciples of Jesus who are going transform their study. I would say we're not your average Christian school. We do things a little bit differently. We have pretty engaging, fun worship time, which is kind of based on some of the experiences I had at SpringHill. Our students learn how to hear God's voice. They learn how to lay hands on people and pray for them. They learn how to give prophetic words to people and minister to them. They take turns leading prophetic singing in the prayer room. They're learning how to really read and study the word of God, but then also pray the word of God over their lives and over their city.

Another familiar aspect of Jessica's school is individualizing the academics to every student:

We do multigrade classrooms, so really it's almost run like homeschool. Every kid is in a different group based on their ability level. It might not be their grade level. Meeting within small groups or one-on-one, everyone is working at their own pace and at their own ability level to make sure they're successful. Probably on average, any new student that comes in, they're two to five grade levels behind in reading, and two to three grade levels behind in math.

After just one year at Jessica's school, her students often grow one and a half to two grade levels. If those kids stay enrolled for two years, Jessica and her staff are usually able to get them to grade level:

I think I'm a lot more fun teacher than teachers in some of these other schools that I did my student teaching with because of everything I experienced at SpringHill. Integrating faith and fun is such a powerful tool, so I implemented a lot of that in my own classroom as a teacher.

SpringHill not only creates life-changing experiences but often leaves behind a lasting impression to do God's work.

That's The SpringHill Experience. Even if our staff members

aren't necessarily people who are going to be educators or working with kids professionally but, instead, end up in business or law or commerce, they have learned leadership. And often times, they have found their purpose.

SpringHill not only creates life-changing experiences but often leaves behind a lasting impression to do God's work.

I think Tyler said it best: "You're able to go deep in fellowship with friends as you serve together. You have a front-row seat to see how God moves in amazing ways."

Reflections on a Summer of Giving Lasts a Lifetime

Where do you turn when the day runs off the tracks, the meeting you've prepared so hard for goes badly, or you're in the middle of that part of your job you dislike the most? What do you do when you're fatigued, worn thin, burned out with your work, with your life? How do you get back that energy you used to have, the joy that filled your work, the motivation to fight through any obstacle?

There's really only one place to turn, one thing you need: to know, believe, and wrap your whole being around your *purpose*. Your purpose answers the question of why you are here. It's the reason you do your job, the reminder of the impact you have, the difference you and your work make, and the outcomes you strive so hard for. It's the reason behind what you do and why you do it.

If you keep your purpose at the forefront of your mind, it provides the energy, joy, and motivation to keep you at your work, to fight through the challenges and boredom. Once you lose your sense of purpose, or worse, you work and live outside the scope of your purpose, your energy, joy, and motivation will soon slip away.

So what exactly is purpose? It's the goals you have, but it's more than numbers or accomplishments. It's the direction you want to go, but it's beyond your destination. Purpose goes deeper, wider, and higher. Purpose is the ultimate end you are seeking for your work, for yourself, and for those you wish to serve. It's who God's called you to be and the good work He's prepared for you to do.

So how do you discover your purpose? You discover it when you clearly understand your highest values, acknowledge your gifts, abilities, and life experiences, and know the opportunities you have to make a difference in the lives of others and in the world. The confluence of knowing yourself and the world you live in is where you discover your purpose.

What circumstances in your youth influenced your course in life? Are you living your purpose? What role did God play in that? What is the relationship between your purpose and your community? How are you helping the children in your life discover their God-given purpose?

CHAPTER SEVEN

The SpringHill Effect at Home

"Sometimes we make things too complicated when we really need to remember that the Kingdom belongs to children." —Heidi Baker

---

The Blessings of Raising Children

- Whether you are a parent or not, you have a hand in raising today's children. Children learn by example, and modeling behavior is something each one of us must be mindful of.

- Parents rely on others to reinforce the lessons and values they teach. Whom do you trust with the children you love? What are the values and perspectives that you want them to have as they grow up?

- What are God's expectations of how we, as a community, raise children?

It was the winter of 2009, right after the fall of 2008, and I'm not just referencing the season. We knew we were going to be struggling to reach our camper numbers. People in Michigan, especially, were reeling from what had happened when the housing market crashed after the Great Recession hit. We were being pretty aggressive in terms of camper recruitment. One of the things we were doing was going to churches and setting up booths and talking to parents.

And one of the directives we settled on for that new year in 2009 was that we would not turn any kids away because mom and dad had lost their job or were struggling financially. We vowed we were going to put kids in the camp, no matter what. Our goal was to make sure people knew that if their kids needed to have The SpringHill Experience, we wanted to make it happen.

On one particular Sunday, we were visiting a church partner, one of our biggest and closest church partners, Kensington Church in metro Detroit. We had set up a booth at the Lake Orion campus, where we talked to parents, passed out brochures, and answered questions, between church services. During the church service, they invited us to go back to the green room for a bite to eat with all the people who were part of the program. As I was standing in the buffet line, one of the staff members approached me to say she wanted me to meet a mom and her daughter.

The mom introduced herself and nine-year-old McKenna.

"McKenna has something she wants to tell you," Mom said.

McKenna proceeded to tell me that she had been at SpringHill for the last couple of summers and absolutely loved it. During the past fall, when the whole economy had crashed, the parents of some of her friends had lost their jobs and some were even losing their homes. She said she wanted to make sure all kids could go to SpringHill, and so she wanted to make a donation. She told me that she had $260 in her savings account and she wanted to give us $240 of it, explaining that she felt she should at least leave $20 in there for a rainy day.

Her mom filled in the blanks and told me how, one night, while McKenna was getting ready for bed and saying her evening prayers, she became very sad to think that kids couldn't go to SpringHill because of what was going on with the economy. She just felt compelled to do something. I remember thinking in that moment that this little girl just brought light and hope into the world. I was incredibly inspired. As I got to know her, I learned quickly that she was one of those people who feel compelled to take action, not just talk.

When I went home and back to the office, I started thinking and praying about what had happened. I knew there were a lot of adults out there who were probably in that year of paralysis, wondering what was going to happen to the economy, what was going to happen to their job. And there was this little girl, in the face of all that, giving away most of her savings.

I called her mom and I asked if she would be okay with me sending a letter to all our supporters to share McKenna's story. What if we could take McKenna's $240 and multiply it and not just get one or two kids into SpringHill, but hundreds and hundreds—like the Bible story of the fishes and the loaves?

Mom was totally on board because part of it was a way to affirm McKenna. I didn't want to simply pat her on the head, I wanted to really affirm her in what she did, to acknowledge that significant moment in her life and her learning. I wanted her to see what can happen when you step out in faith and are generous.

So we wrote a letter, a really personal letter, to our supporters. I addressed the economic times and the pain and difficulties that so many people were going through, and I shared the story of McKenna. I asked them to consider matching her gift to make it grow.

When all was said and done, we raised $100,000 for scholarships.

No act of kindness or compassion is ever too small in God's eyes.

The money just kept rolling in. It was absolutely incredible. McKenna got to see what her step of faith did, and it was kind of like the stone that starts an avalanche. I think it really brought hope too. It allowed us to also live out our conviction of not turning kids away just because of tough times. We figure out how to raise the necessary funds.

McKenna continued to come back to SpringHill. Now she's in college. We've had those conversations with her and her family about the significant role that SpringHill and that moment of compassion have played in her life. I remember, when she was young, she'd write me these really adorable notes. I'd probably get one a couple of times a year:

"P.S. Remember I want your job one day!"

That would be great, McKenna. Let's get you ready for that, I'd think.

A Partnership with Parents

What we try to do at SpringHill, our mission, is about creating life-impacting experiences for kids—and their families. For us, it really is not just about somebody making a faith commitment or raising a hand at the end of a message. It really is about a transformation of somebody's life, a change, a turn. It's really tangible. That integration of faith and fun is just part of The SpringHill Experience and The SpringHill Way.

"From day one every single person from SpringHill was energized and pumped up to be at camp. Very nicely organized, and you could tell the counselors wanted to be with the kids. I loved how all the directors and counselors greeted us each morning also! The best part was the last day of camp when each child got a character award and was recognized and told in front of the whole group why they received that award. That, to me, is better than any grade in school."
—SpringHill Parent

When parents say, "Why should we send our kid to SpringHill?" The answer is that, yes, they will have a great time and learn about the Gospel, but what we're really trying to do is transform their lives, make a turn, a change. And though we think of ourselves as serving parents and families, we really see it in terms of partnering with them. We're joining with them to help them, just as we would think about a partnership with a church. We want to help them accomplish their goals and dreams for their kids.

And so I think, with that in mind, what it really means is that we work hard to create this level of trust with parents. Obviously, there's the first level of trust: we will take care of their kids; they will be safe. But then we go the extra mile to make sure our staff are trained in the most up-to-date safety and risk management procedures. The next level is about the spiritual and moral trust that our kids' parents have come to place in us, and about our aligning with them in terms of their values, who they are, and what they want for their kids.

We try to earn that trust on those two levels. The first one is the foundation. But the second one is really where the buy-in happens. It's what makes people choose SpringHill over other options. And I'm not talking about camps, per se. I'm talking about any option parents have for their kids in the summertime.

Parents feel they have an ally in SpringHill, a partner right there beside them, raising their kids.

As a matter of fact, one of our old taglines going back into the 1970s was: "SpringHill helps parents raise good kids."

Parents feel they have an ally in SpringHill, a partner right there beside them, raising their kids.

"This day camp was the best-run children's experience any of my eight kids have participated in. The staff was enthusiastic and energetic. They took time to really *look* at the kids they were working with, as evidenced by the awards the last day. SpringHill's emphasis on kindness, and circumventing potential bullying was very refreshing." —SpringHill Parent

---

One of the greatest sources of pride for us is when we hear from parents over and over that they trust us. We've become a second voice for them, speaking the same messages, role-modeling the same values. Our new, fresh voice reinforces all they have been teaching at home. The kids may have heard Mom and Dad say things and live out how to behave and how to live, But when they go away to camp and see these college students and other young adults talking about the same things and living out the same behaviors, it's extremely impactful.

Take, for instance, a mom such as Shelly Johnson, who was so afraid to send her three sons away to camp. As a freelance journalist, she did painstaking research, and she was so glad she overcame initial reservations. For SpringHill, she says, imbued her sons with faith and wisdom well beyond their years, and they begged her to send them back. She did and has done every year since. She gives thanks to God for the foresight to send them to SpringHill. They talk about how much fun they had and how the counselors became big brothers and friends and mentors who drew them nearer to God. And all three boys love telling their mom Bible stories they learned at SpringHill.

Emily Streeter speaks eloquently of what seemed a miracle: Her rebellious son, disobedient, disrespectful, and selfish, returned home from SpringHill a radically changed boy. Emily and her husband asked, a few weeks later, why he had begun obeying them and suddenly getting along with his four siblings. "Well," he told his parents, "I realized if I can obey my counselor who only really knows me for a week, I should be able to obey my parents who love me so much more." Emily marvels at the transformation over a matter of weeks. "SpringHill," she says, "changed our family for the better."

The parents of children with special needs find The SpringHill Experience a unique kind of blessing. I found this out during one of my parent survey calls. One mother in particular had given us a super positive rating, and so I asked her why she sent her kids to SpringHill. She said she had a son with Down syndrome, and he just loved our camp.

"Our first thing we schedule every year is to have our kids come," she said. "He loves it so much that the past school year, he had to do a presentation in class, and he did his on SpringHill and his experiences there. His classmates helped him put a PowerPoint presentation together, the whole nine yards. That's how much he loved it."

So, we just talked about it, the experience. It was a great conversation. Then I got to my last question.

"Is there anything we could do better for you or for your son to improve the experience, or improve how we interact with him?"

"No, I don't think so. We just love it so much. It's just so awesome," she replied.

I wasn't taking no for an answer. "Now, there's got to be something we can do. Help us. We want to be better. Help us to do this. Holy discontent is one of our core values."

"Let me think," she said, and became very quiet. I can hear her starting to sniffle on the phone, and she starts to cry. "There is one thing you can do. If he could be there for two weeks—we always only get a week."

The thing is we have this really long waiting list of kids, like her son, who want to come to SpringHill. Before I could say anything, she said, "You know, we had him go to another camp. It's a camp for kids with special needs, and it was a fine camp. They treated him well. It was good; he had fun. But it's not SpringHill. He loves SpringHill because he gets to be with all the other kids. He gets to be a regular kid. You need to know having to parent a child with special needs—how difficult it is, how draining, and how much work it is. To have a two-week respite where we know he's having the time of his life, yet we're not caring for him, is just huge for our family."

By then, I was choking up as well. "You know what? I'd love to figure out how to have him here two weeks next year. Let me go to work to see if we can make that happen."

Her response? She just screamed and handed over the phone to her son. Suddenly, I was on the phone with him, and he was thanking me for letting him come for two weeks. Needless to say, it was kind of a done deal at that point.

Parents need partners to raise children. They need a village—support—and to know they are not alone.

Rough Beginnings, Happy Endings

Parents need partners to raise children. They need a village—support—and to know they are not alone.

But the warm and fuzzy feelings don't always start off that way. I was at an opening day at our camp in Michigan a number of years ago. I usually stand in a spot where I can see parents coming and going, dropping kids off, doing the tour, and then going to their cars. I watched a mom step off one of our tour wagons. I was probably forty yards from her, but I could tell she did not look happy.

I thought, *Oh no! What happened?*

She had gone to see her son at his cabin. When she got off the tour wagon, she literally marched toward her car. I watched her get halfway there, turn around, and march my way. There was definitely something going on.

As she came closer, I said, "What can I do for you?"

"I really have problem and I want you to fix it," she said. "I saw my son in his cabin and there is a kid that is disabled in there. He clearly has issues, emotional or mental issues, and he's in that cabin with my son. He should not be in there. He is going to ruin my son's week at camp."

"Well, you know we have an inclusion program at SpringHill," I said. "It's really clear on our website. We include all kids in the cabins, and we'll do whatever we can to make sure that campers with special needs have an awesome week, as well as the kids in the camp with them. We will not allow his special needs to hinder your son's experience."

She wasn't having it. "It's not fair. It puts pressure on him to have to interact"

"I promise you we won't allow it to affect his time here," I said.

But she was somehow convinced that just having the special-needs child in the same cabin with her son was going to create an issue. Finally, she asked me to move the kid with special needs to a different cabin.

"I'm sorry," I said calmly. "I can't do that, and I'm not going to do that. That's not going to happen. That's not how we do things here."

"Well then, I'll take my kid home and I want my money back!"

So I said, "Let's do this: I'll make you a deal. You leave your kid here this week. You pick him up on Friday. If he's had a terrible week because of that other camper, we'll give you your money back. You come see me on Friday when you pick him up, and you let me know, and we'll refund you right on the spot."

Next Friday came, and of course, her son had the best week of his life. And Mom personally apologized.

I've found that all parents, even those who had been reluctant to send their kids off to camp, come to see SpringHill as a godsend for their children's spiritual, emotional, and social development. At the end of the day, it really isn't about making SpringHill great, or SpringHill looking good in our kids' or families' eyes.

It's really about how we create this place for God to do this kind of work.

It's really about how we create this place for God to do this kind of work.

Reflections on The SpringHill Effect at Home

I'm convinced that, after twenty-six years of being a parent, the key responsibility we have as parents, maybe the only responsibility, is to lead our children. This may seem obvious, but the truth is many parents don't lead, either because they don't know how to or simply don't believe it's their place. But the truth is the very first social organizations in history were not businesses, nonprofits, or governments. They were *families*. And since healthy organizations require leadership, we shouldn't be surprised that healthy families need leadership, and that every child needs to be led.

So what are the ways parents can lead their child?

Parents have the same options available as leaders of any organization: they can push, drag, carry, or inspire their children. Maybe, the only difference is that for parents, especially parents of young children and adolescents, it's appropriate to use all four ways more often than when leading adults. As a result, the key to successful parenting is having the wisdom to know when to lead and which way to lead.

Unfortunately, this is usually where we parents make mistakes. We push when we should carry, we carry when we should inspire, and we drag when a gentle nudge is all that is needed.

And just as with leading teams, parents (me included) can fall into one way of leading because it worked so well at one particular moment or season in our child's life. The tricky part is to be able to recognize the need to move away from a specific approach when the child's ready to be led differently. My wife and I have seen this in the parenting of our own children, who are now adults. When they were children, we often dragged them to piano practice, pushed them to eat right, and carried them when life was beyond their capacity to handle it. But when they are adults, our children don't appreciate being pushed, dragged, and most often, carried. They do want to be inspired, however. So, a new season in our children's life requires a shift in the way we parent.

How do we know we're parenting the best way? Our children should be accomplishing both our short-term goals (eating their vegetables) and our long-term goals (becoming people who don't need to be pushed, pulled, or carried).

So this leaves us with the question we all face as parents: Are we ready to give up our go-to parenting ways for the better way at this particular time in our child's life? What other voices are the children in your life listening to? Are they the voices you want them to hear, with the messages that you value? If it is true it takes a community to raise a child, what kind of community should it be? Who should be part of that community?

CHAPTER EIGHT

Beyond SpringHill

"God has given each of you a gift. Use it to help each other. This will show God's loving favor."
—1 Peter 4:10

Finding Hope and Support in the Community

- Being relationally focused, we know an investment in others offers a return beyond comprehension. How do you invest in your relationships?

- We could never do the things we do or have an impact on the lives of others were it not for critical relationships in our community. How do you connect your successes to the relationships you've built?

- Building relationships is like planting seeds. When the harvest comes, we are blessed abundantly with love and support. Think back to when you planted the seeds of relationships and reaped the rewards.

One of the first things I learned in my introduction to economics class back at Central Michigan University was that economics is best described as the tension between "unlimited wants and limited resources." This perfectly describes the tension we experience at SpringHill every fall as we finish our upcoming year's financial plan, or what we affectionately call "the budget."

It's an all-hands-on-deck, or should I say, all-brains-on-deck, kind of activity because of the importance we place on the entire team's input and ultimate ownership of the financial plan. It tends to be a time when everyone's brain hurts while passions and frustrations run high.

The financial plan is the final step in the development of our Annual Ministry Plan, which includes which SpringHill experiences we'll offer and to whom, where we'll offer these experiences, and the anticipated number of participants. We also work out the details of everything we'll need to carry out these experiences, including capital investment and staffing. Finally, we align this plan with our three-year strategic plan to be sure we're headed in the right direction and accomplishing our long-term goals.

"I have followed SpringHill and watched the ministry progress over the years. SpringHill is ready to expand to new parts of the country. The plan is rock solid, sustainable, and the growth resulting from it will expose thousands of young people to the message of Jesus Christ. The spiritual ROI on SpringHill's growth will be high. I'm in." —Bill Payne, Vice Chairman, Amway (Ada, Michigan)

We dream big for God, which results in big plans early in the process. Then we begin to put dollars and cents to these plans and the tension begins to rise because our dreams are always unlimited but, we discover, God generally gives us limited resources. Over the years, I've become convinced that God does this so that our big plans become His plans.

SpringHill relies on generous donations to make the rich camping experience possible for children with special needs, foster children, and poor, urban kids who cannot otherwise afford camp. More than 400 campers a year attend SpringHill through named scholarships alone. These include the Africa La Calle Memorial Fund, David Neeld Fund, Elijah's Cloak God's Protection through the Storm scholarship, Jesse Buist Memorial Scholarship, Noah's Fund Special-Needs Scholarship, Urban Hope Scholarship, and West Michigan Scholarships.

"SpringHill has become a role model to these kids. They understand the big picture. I go home into their neighborhood and see them outside. I see them get in a huddle on the basketball court and they will remember how SpringHill did things and related activities back to God. These kids look forward to seeing this camp come every year. Camp is not just us impacting them; it's them impacting us." — Kevin, Day Camp Counselor

---

So we get to do what we do well, which is create this experience The SpringHill Way, and the church gets to do what it does well, which is build relationships, invest in the community, and invest in the lives of those people.

We have a group of stakeholders we call donors. And really, *donors* is a broad term for us. It means people, obviously, who contribute financially, whether it's big or small—any kind of financial contribution. Little McKenna and the Van Halls are examples of donors. And little did I realize the extent to which being a donor was a reciprocal relationship. Darlene Van Hall says it best:

> When you talk about the SpringHill Experience, it's an experience for us too. We're sixty-plus years old and could retire, but years ago, our attorney advised us not to. He said, "Why retire when you can make money and donate to worthy causes." I think that started our process, thinking that was a very good idea. Why not? We don't need more for ourselves. We have so much. Besides, it's really not ours to begin with. The longer Arvin and I talked about this, the more we realized it's all God. We are using it on loan from God. So every time we get a book about SpringHill, every time we send someone to camp there, or every time we talk to Michael, it's a SpringHill Experience for us.

High-school sweethearts Arvin and Darlene started their business, Skunk River Block and Pallet, in 1979, with a Sears air compressor, a nail gun, and an old sawmill. They built pallets, and that business just grew and grew. But on the morning of July 2, 2011, they got a phone call that their family business was on fire. By the time they got there, it was fully engulfed, and before long, had burned completely to the ground.

Arvin says something divine happened then. "Nobody got hurt. Records that were just in cardboard boxes sitting below a computer that had melted didn't get hurt. Stuff like that makes you say, 'That's just crazy. How did that happen?' The fire broke out in February, and by Thanksgiving we moved back in and were up and running. This was a $1.8 million fire. We said right away that God must have a passion or a reason for us to get this thing back up and running—to make sure we do good things … Last year was a record year."

> "I have had a lot of adventures making new friends and having fun with people—adventures like climbing with friends up Spider Mountain. It was fun because you had to go through many obstacles, pushing through webs and hauling yourself up. The webs felt like sin and we had to push through it." —Eli

Darlene explains their experience:

SpringHill is such a great organization. The people who are the leaders just have a way of connecting, a way with people, a way of helping others. We're all blessed to be a blessing. I think that's our theory about life, our philosophy. God has blessed us so richly that we are just blessed to be able to be in connection with SpringHill through the years, and to be a blessing to so many other people.

As you walk on the grounds of SpringHill, there's just a spirituality feeling of God being present there. I think that was important for us too. Just feeling the Holy Spirit leading, not only the leaders, but also for the kids' sake, and for us as we walked over the grounds. It's being prayed for all the time, and you can just feel that. You can feel God's presence. Our oldest granddaughter, Elissa, this will be her third time at camp this year.

Last year, she had gone to camp in June, and in August we took her to Minnesota on a little fishing vacation with us on the boat. As I was putting her life jacket on, she said, "Nana, do you realize I learned this at camp: that God is our life jacket also?" I said, "Really?" She replied, "It keeps us from sinking. And just like the life jacket keeps us from sinking in the water, God keeps us from sinking into our sins." I was stunned. I just said, "Really." I had chills, and I had goosebumps, and I had to call Michael right away and tell him whatever he was doing really works!

Arvin adds:

We just feel like all kids should have the same opportunity. We're all born into this world equal. But some kids just do not have the same opportunities, and we just feel like SpringHill is such a great resource that connects kids to Christ, that connects kids to something more. That connection with God is such an important tool. We see that as kids get so busy in life, you have to grasp them at a certain age or it gets harder and harder the older they get.

If they get a week away from whatever they're dealing with, and they are surrounded by love and caring people. You know, it's probably kind of like an electric shock. It sends them back out into the world knowing there is something better and, hopefully, gives them something to take with them to help them get through whatever they might be going through.

Arvin and Darlene are extremely gracious, amazing people, and over the years, they have become very dear friends. They are also very private. They don't ask for recognition. They don't want their names in lights. That kind of pomp and circumstance just isn't important to them. They simply want to be able to give and glorify God with what they can.

"The best recognition we have is on Colin's Ridge. There's a piece of gas pipe stuck up there, a little gas fitting, because that's how the whole thing got started," says Arvin.

Darlene makes an astute comparison. "At the time, we were helping our son move into his home. We needed something to be fixed. The stove was broken down and we needed it to be fixed. I equate that to our lives too. We're all broken, and just by looking at that little piece of pipe, we're always reminded that our lives need fixing. So that's why I think it's such an awesome story, and how God has such a hand in all of this."

The night we dedicated Colin's Ridge, Colin and his parents stayed there, and so did Arvin and Darlene. The next morning, Colin's mom told the Van Halls that because the facilities inside are designed for special-needs people, her son, for the first time in his life, could wheel himself up to a sink and brush his own teeth. As Darlene describes it:

> She told me that all the other sinks—you just couldn't get there in a wheelchair, and Colin is confined to a wheelchair. She had tears in her eyes, like I do now. But to hear something so simple as being able to brush your teeth yourself for the first time in your life—can you imagine? God keeps using us in ways we don't understand. Our sermon last weekend was God sends mysteries in life and miracles in life, and we have to get to know God through

both of these. And that's, I think, the most important thing that we can carry in our hearts. There are a lot of mysteries in life, but there are a lot of miracles too.

At SpringHill, we know people have more to give than money. So we also consider our volunteers as stakeholders. We use volunteers to do work at our camp properties and run our day camp experiences. We even have families that host our staff when we're in certain cities. Volunteers are a key part of what we do.

And then we have our prayer partners, people we pray with. Literally, we have a list of 10,000 people who get our prayer list and are committed to praying for SpringHill and whatever is going on at SpringHill. We consider that a sacred kind of relationship.

We also have a group of stakeholders we call our ambassadors. These are people who are loyal fans, who spread the word, who promote us, who tell their family and friends about SpringHill and what we're doing, and they recruit their own kids and family members to attend SpringHill experiences.

We even have a group on Facebook called The SpringHill Squad. It's a group of parents who love SpringHill, share their experiences, and promote us.

And then there are others who are a combination of all of the above—people such as Mike Smith.

Building Relationships That Last a Lifetime

In 1994 Mike and his wife, Deecy, formed a company called Designvox, a design firm that really started out as a studio offering communications design services. Having, initially, recruited clients in the furniture industry, their client list now includes Ford, Whirlpool, Steelcase, OFS, Cummings Diesel, and Eli Lilly. They serve their clients' needs behind the scenes, doing strategic design work related to communications and culture change, specifically health and well-being.

Also nestled among their clients is SpringHill.

They've been instrumental in all the SpringHill branding, helping to nurture it and hold it to a certain place, a certain standard. But Mike's ties to SpringHill don't end there. Nor did they begin there.

Back in 1969, during SpringHill's very first summer, Mike was a nine-year-old camper. His father had a job as a game warden in the area, and he wanted to help Enoch get the fledgling, innovative camp off the ground by taking care of the environmental sides of things. So he ended up assisting the staff with duties such as planting trees, and was instrumental in helping SpringHill get our rifle range built. Whenever his father had meetings at SpringHill, Mike would tag along.

And for the next seven years, Mike called SpringHill home during the summer and describes it as follows:

> As a twelve-year-old in 1972, I can remember a significant realization of a need for not only faith, but a need to have a committed life to Christ, and what that really meant. I can remember thinking that SpringHill was more than just going to church, more than just spending time around other people who believed what I believed. It was about taking responsibility for a personal relationship with God, and all such a commitment entailed.

When he turned sixteen, he started on the staff as a canoe instructor, and he stayed on for several more years. "I would come back every summer on staff to do a number of different jobs. While I worked there, I developed a lot of relationships with both friends and with the leadership."

As I had, Mike befriended both Enoch and his son, Mark. In fact,

Mark became a very close friend of Mike's when he was a freshman in college, as the two became housemates. Mark was going to Calvin, while Mike was attending a design school nearby. As Mike says:

> I remember Mark coming to me when I was probably nineteen years old and asking if I would be an area director for the summer. I was planning on being a counselor, but they needed an area director. When I think about the leadership choices that I've been involved in, the decisions that he and Enoch made, the trust that SpringHill placed in me—they saw things in me that I didn't see in myself as a young adult, and that was pivotal for me in terms of everything moving forward from that point. The decisions that I made each and every day, the confidence that I had to lead people, all of it helped shape my life.

It was that sort of trust Enoch and his team placed in people that was life changing for so many. One summer, Enoch hired a waterfront director, who would oversee all of the lifeguards, a young man named Dennis, who was a swimmer at Central Michigan University.

Enoch added that young man to the team, giving him a very critical position, yet knowing that Dennis didn't have a deep faith. But Enoch saw in him the potential and the hunger for God. During staff training, which was the week before camp, he really felt that Dennis would be worth investing in, and that process continued throughout the summer. Enoch's investment was returned tenfold, as Dennis, eventually, made the decision to follow Christ. From that point on, a very significant part of his life shifted and changed. As Mike says:

> And I can remember moments like that where the investment in people and individuals, not just in the kids, but in the staff, made a huge impact on me. There were just these

amazing connections to people that Enoch and Mark were able to create. They had the ability to extract the authenticity and the integrity from those individuals, to pull out their different gifts, different abilities, different talents, but all with a high degree of integrity, and all while reinforcing the desire to have as many kids as possible hear the gospel message and understand who Jesus is.

Mike Smith also remembers the day I asked him to consider joining the board of directors for SpringHill. It was the year after Mark had passed away, and I was aware of Mike's love, passion, and commitment to our ministry. In Mike's own words:

> What attracted me the most was the consistency of the vision of the organization, and the commitment of the leadership to make sure that we were always trying to share the message of Christ with as many young people as possible. That, along with the idea of not getting comfortable, our core value of holy discontent, of constant growth, and exploring new things and new ideas. Part of what I've seen change over the years has been the fact that some of the methods are slightly tweaked. The whole day camp concept, the idea of leadership development, and some of the other things that we are going to prototype with the gap-year program, those types of things are different. But at the end of the day, nothing has changed. It's still all about reaching more kids with the message of Christ.

> But a big part of it also is not limiting ourselves to say we're just a camp. And I think that's one of the hardest things to capture and convey. People who have a significant experience at a place tend to hold that place in reverence. Now,

it's true that a place is an important part of creating an environment to help people be open to change, and to be interested in the things that you have to say. The reality has actually been proven now with our day camps going into metro Detroit, by sharing the gospel in a slightly different place and yet trying to create the experience where kids come to know Christ better and know him fully in addition to understanding the gospel. It's like the message hasn't changed, the methods haven't even changed, but I would say that we're much more open to the types of opportunities that align with that vision, what's the best way to reach kids and to help them grow in Christ.

Our firm has been a tremendous blessing to so many creative people. We're kind of built around the idea, this very SpringHill-like idea, that a team of creative thinkers can really come up with something that none of the individuals by themselves could ever come up with. In other words, what we're able to accomplish as a group, as a diverse team of diverse thinkers is much more meaningful and rich, and usually more effective, than what any of the individuals can sit down and come up with on their own.

Not only is Mike Smith a former camper and staff member, and current board member and supporter, but all five of his children started going to SpringHill as soon as they were old enough. Two of them have worked there, one as a special-needs counselor and one as a photographer. His son with Down syndrome started going to SpringHill when he was seven, just as his siblings did, and witnessed firsthand the ability to embrace diversity in a world where, oftentimes, kids with special needs are considered the most marginalized. Mike talks about this aspect of SpringHill as follows:

> Yet to include them fully into the program, into a community, into the environment of SpringHill, that is one of the best gifts that SpringHill could give. And it has had a huge impact in our family. I've also seen it have a huge impact in kids' lives as they've embraced kids with special needs. My kids had the *privilege* to grow up with their brother. A lot of kids who got to know Connor once he was in their cabin, they got the benefit of understanding and compassion, and could be more comfortable with kids with differences. They realized they had nothing to be afraid of. They didn't have to treat him any certain way. Because he was just like them, with the same needs we all have. That's an area I've been really committed to, and in that I've been really proud of Michael to be such a strong supporter. The full inclusion of kids has really been an exciting area.
>
> Because if you spend any time with parents who have kids with special needs, a lot of times they are the only advocates for their children. And there's a lot of aloneness in that. You're fighting with the schools constantly to get the best services for your kid. You're fighting with the state to get the best opportunities for them and their care. It's a very interesting dynamic. It's kind of behaving the way the church should behave in terms of embracing and including and bringing in and pulling a community together.

The impact of SpringHill is more than personal, it's generational. One of the things that we've also done that has been very intentional is that we've tried to partner with other like-minded organizations.

They could be businesses, for-profit organizations, other camps, or other youth ministries. We've been really intentional about that, partly because, in our vision, we talk about wanting to be a pioneering ministry, which means we see pioneers as people who go to new places and blaze new trails, and we wanted to blaze trails others could follow.

The impact of SpringHill is more than personal, it's generational.

We want to be an influential ally. We want to partner with others whom we can help to become better and more effective at what they do. Today there are organizations like ours around the world that organize day camps as we do. Why? Because we have helped them. We not only gave them the idea but have, literally, walked with them and consulted with them, all for free. There's a camp in New Zealand that is now offering day camps. There's a camp in Canada. There are tens of thousands of kids beyond SpringHill who are having this local day camp experience because we've helped these organizations launch day camps.

And we continue to support. We've created a peer group made up of these organizations that meets once a year. The leaders of the day camps go there to talk about what's working and what's not. Again, it's an attitude of inclusion: we're in this together. This isn't competition; this is God's work.

Our creativity, that innovation, that pioneering—we've always had this history of creating unique housing areas, or unique activities. We created an industry for portable climbing walls and the Eurobungy. We, literally, helped design and create what's out there. We don't market them or sell them, but we've been the key influencer.

"I liked the Eurobungy because you get to do flips and completely trust God the whole way. When I was on it, I had to rely and pray to God that He would get me down safely. That is like all the activities at camp and I love that about SpringHill. When I go home, I will be different. I learned lots about Jesus at campfire last night and I want everyone to hear what I heard last night … This is something I can't keep to myself and just here." —Dylan

---

If you go to overnight camps around the world, you'll see glimpses of SpringHill. My wife and I were in Spain recently, at a conference where we were both teaching. It was a Christian camping conference, and we had been invited by a guy named David Frank.

David Frank used to work for SpringHill in the 1970s, and when he left, he and his wife became missionaries in Europe. They tried to plant churches in Spain and realized it wasn't working really well, but they found what really worked was camps.

So they purchased a camp called La'Arcada. And you want to know what you find when you go to La'Arcada? They have teepees. They have American Indian legends and stories and themes everywhere. And they got it from SpringHill.

Because of one of our core values is to be relationally focused, we connect with all these people and try to relate to them in a personal way. We feel they're part of the SpringHill family, and we really do see them as partners in doing this work for kids.

I think the way God made SpringHill, where we really are dependent on our partners to do what we do, is nothing short of amazing. They need us, but we definitely need them. We need our donors. We need those ambassadors who will speak on our behalf. We need those volunteers on the weekends. There's no way we could do it without those volunteers who are working on the tubing hill, working in the dining hall, and working up in the game room. We just don't have enough marketing dollars. We don't have enough money to hire all the staff, and we don't price our services so that we have enough margin to award scholarships to kids.

God's made us so that we need to have these relationships to do what we do. And I think it's a really great position to be in because it keeps us dependent on God first but dependent on those relationships as well.

We provide a place for people to live out their sense of calling, or their desire to make a difference.

Reflections on Beyond SpringHill

"It's not what you know but who you know that counts," is one of those maxims that can be difficult to swallow, especially for those of us who value performance over politics. But the reality is there's a kernel of truth in this maxim, especially when thinking about it in terms of relationships rather than politics.

You see, relationships do matter, and more often than not, they're the tipping point in any given situation or decision. Healthy relationships, whether personal or professional, will always carry the day, even in those moments when everything falls apart.

And relationships are not only good at saving the day but also essential in building teams that can accomplish extraordinary things. Very rarely have history-changing ideas, projects, or efforts been accomplished solo. Almost always, great moments have been created by teams of people working in the context of personal, loving, and caring relationships.

So what does it take to create healthy relationships? There are two simple ingredients:

1. To know, and

2. To be known.

Teddy Roosevelt once said, "People don't care how much you know until they know how much you care." Relationships require knowing others, who they are, what's important to them, their history, their stories, and how we can assist them and their goals. Relationships require us to think of others first and so see the world through their eyes, and in the end, to simply and deeply *know* the other person.

Healthy and meaningful relationships also require us *to be known*: allowing others to see into our lives, to know our thoughts, our hopes, and our dreams. To be known in this way is foundational to building the kind of relationships necessary for teams that change the world. Without transparency, there's no possibility of trust. Without trust there's no true relationship. Where there's no true relationship, there's no team or community. And where there's no team or community, the possibility of world-changing actions diminishes to almost zero.

When looking at your own personal and professional relationships, are you *known*? Do you truly *know* those you work and live with on a day-to-day basis? How can you become more involved in helping the children in you life learn this type of relationship building with others? How about with God? What would the world look like if children were to grow up with faith-based relationships and fully lived-out Christ-like values? Can you name any investment more important than the investment in the spiritual development of children?

EPILOGUE

For the Kids

"Some believe it is only great power that can hold evil in check, but that is not what I have found. It is the small everyday deeds of ordinary folk that keep the darkness at bay. Small acts of kindness and love." —J. R. R. Tolkien, *The Lord of the Rings*

There once was a horse who lived on a farm with other farm animals. There were two goats, three sheep, a pig, a handful of chickens, and a milk cow. Each of these animals was an important part of the livelihood of the farm family, the MacDonalds, providing food and other products for use and trade. Now, as most people know, horses are the smartest of all the farm animals, and this horse was no exception. As a matter of fact, she was smarter than the average horse, having the ability to simply look at a situation and find a solution to address it.

A situation arose one day that required all the intelligence the horse could muster: the entire MacDonald family fell ill of a contagious disease and was unable to care for the farm and its animals. Eggs needed to be collected, the pig fed, the cow and goats milked, the sheep sheared, the barnyard cleaned, and the fences mended, yet the family was incapable of doing any of it. So the horse began to devise a plan to help the MacDonalds by taking care of the farm. But it soon became clear that as smart as the horse was, she could not devise a plan that assured all the farm chores were done in a timely and orderly manner.

As the hours and days began to slip by, the situation became dire. The farm was becoming chaotic and, as anyone who has spent time on a farm knows, chaos is the last word that should describe a farm. Finally, in desperation, the horse began to do the farm work herself. She tried to collect the hens' eggs but found she dropped them too often, or accidently broke them in her teeth. She attempted to feed the pig but couldn't stomach the smell of the mush. She even tried to milk the cow and the goats but got kicked because her hoofs hurt their udders too much. Instead of helping the MacDonalds, the horse was making the situation worse. It seemed the more she tried to do herself, the worse the farm became. She was desperate to help but didn't know what to do.

Then, when things were at their lowest point, the pig came to the horse and said:

> I know you want to help the MacDonalds, but so do I and so do all the other farm animals. If for no other reason than to make sure there are no more broken eggs rotting in the barnyard, or udders rubbed raw. You see, it's in our best interest as well to have the farm taken care of. But you haven't asked for our help. You haven't allowed us to do the work we're capable of doing. Instead you've tried to do it all yourself.

Even though I'm not as intelligent as you, I'm very hungry and that's driven me to think about and devise this recommendation. First, because you're the oldest and smartest animal in the farm, you need to be our leader. As our leader, you must bring all the animals together and explain the situation so we're all in the same pen together and then you must ask for our help. Lead us in figuring out the work only we can do because we have the gifts, abilities, and experience to do it right and on time. Finally, support and encourage us in our work. Assist us in moving any rocks that stand in our way, help us think through difficult situations, and make sure we're all working together.

If you can lead us in this way I'm sure we can help you bring order back to our farm. But if you insist on doing all the work yourself, the situation will continue to get worse and we'll all suffer, including the MacDonalds.

So the horse listened to the pig and carried out his recommendation. And before long, the farm started to turn around. The chickens decided to lay their eggs right in the egg baskets, thus avoiding extra handling. The cow milked the goats and the goats milked the cow since both understood the delicate and sensitive work that milking is. And the pig started to clean the barnyard of all the rotting eggs and other debris, bringing order to the yard and, at the same time, fixing himself a fine meal.

It was such a remarkable turn-around that the horse began to write in her journal all the lessons she had learned from this experience so she'd never forget them (a practice all smart horses do in these situations). The first lesson the horse recorded was to never prejudge an animal by its looks or the food it eats. (Pigs can and often have great ideas. You just need to ask and listen to them.)

The second lesson was this: every animal has different gifts, abilities, and experiences and so is capable of doing different and important work. The job of the leader is to get to know each member of the farm community in order to understand each animal's capacity to contribute, and then help all the animals to do so.

Lesson three was simply remembering it's almost always in the best interest of everyone involved in a bad situation to see the situation improve, so everyone will be motivated to do something to make a difference. A leader's responsibility is to recognize this interest, and then motivate and channel productive work.

The final lesson the horse wrote down in her journal was simply this: self-realization. Leaders must do only what they, as leaders, *can do*. A leader must stay the course and not try do the things someone else is more capable of doing, or more motivated to do. And one of those things only a leader can do is help others identify what unique skills they have and allow them to flourish in doing what only they can do.

That's always been my focus as the president of SpringHill: leading by surrounding myself with others who thrive on doing the things I can't do, encouraging, guiding, and supporting them in their own God-given talents, and helping them grow, personally and professionally, because I know we're all looking to fulfill the mission of the farm—or should I say, of SpringHill?

Leadership and strategic thinking isn't about having all the answers. At its core, it's about asking the right questions and then leading a team or organization to discover the best answers. And these answers are critical because it's around them that a leader builds unity, community, focus, and ultimately, success.

The following groups of questions are the most foundational and strategic questions leaders can ask and then help their team, or organization, to answer:

1. **Why do we exist?** What purpose do we fulfill, what difference do we make in the world? If we ceased to exist, what hole would be left? The answer to these questions is, typically, expressed in a purpose or mission statement. At SpringHill, we answer this question with our mission: "To glorify God by creating life-impacting experiences where young people can come to know Jesus Christ and grow in their relationship with Him."

   The SpringHill Experience is the tangible expression and evidence of our mission. When we create this experience for the kids, we're fulfilling our mission. From a marketing viewpoint, The SpringHill Experience is our brand.

2. **What's most important to us?** What are we most deeply passionate about and willing to sacrifice and suffer for? The answers to these questions are stated as an organization's core values. At SpringHill we answer this question with an acronym we have for our core values: ARCH, which stands for adventurous faith, relationally focused, contagious joy, and holy discontent. These core values define the kind of organization we are, as well as how we work with each other and all our stakeholder groups: kids, families, allies, donors, and staff (KFADS). Others should see all four of these values lived out within SpringHill.

   The SpringHill Way is the tangible expression of our core values. It's our core values made actionable. It's how we live out our core values in a programmatic way. It's our very intentional and specific approach to creating experiences. From a marketing standpoint, The SpringHill Way is what makes us different from everyone else. Many organizations have similar missions, values, and even brand promises, but it's how we deliver these that makes us different.

Last year, when our summer ended, we said goodbye to 27,000 children and teens and 1,100 young adult leaders in over 135 SpringHill locations throughout eight states. Yes, at SpringHill, we pack 80 percent of our direct missional work into four months.

From the middle of May until the final SpringHill Experience is finished in the middle of August, I feel as though I'm shouldering a great weight: the responsibility for the lives of all these people. But at the same time, I've also just lived four months off the inspiration and energy that comes from working with such an amazing, embracing, talented, committed, and diverse SpringHill community: professional staff who worked hard the prior eight months to have us ready for summer and then served tirelessly almost every day, all day, for four straight months. They work alongside our summer leaders, who give up their summer to serve kids unselfishly, with great love, energy, and passion, and alongside our volunteers, ambassadors, and supporters, who host, paint, drive trams, serve in our medical centers, provide meals, garden, and work in the offices, helping us create SpringHill Experiences.

As happens when finishing a long race, or accomplishing a significant goal, or coming off any adrenaline high, finishing a SpringHill summer means coming off the mountain. It means adapting to a new season of planning and steady work, looking ahead to what's next.

Writing this book has allowed me to look back over the past twenty years and to remember and reflect on remarkable stories, people, relationships, learning, and growth. I allow myself to bask in all of these for a while, and I'm always looking for ways to make the next summer the best yet. This forward look provides me with new energy to tackle this next season with enthusiasm.

So, as we tell kids at SpringHill, you can't stay on the mountain forever; you have to go back home. For us too, SpringHill summers don't last forever. We have to go back home (or to the office), and begin hosting retreats and getting ready for another summer. There's new work to be done, places to go, people to meet. Next summer will be here before we know it, and we'll have another opportunity to experience it all over again.

I may lead, but it is truly our stakeholders, our KFADS, who make all this happen. The focus of our mission is the kids. That's why they're listed first. The other four stakeholders form a missional community (relationally focused) to serve these kids. In the perfect SpringHill world, this missional community aligns with the hopes and dreams of the kids (The SpringHill Experience) and how we'll create those experiences (The SpringHill Way).

I picture the four stakeholders locked arm in arm in a circle, with the kids in the middle.

We're all working together to create a life transformation, The SpringHill Experience, The SpringHill Way.

And in the end that's our desire: our plans will be God's plans because we want the results and the glory to be all His.

At the end of the day, it's all about FTK.

No, the letters FTK are not a secret code, and yes, they have meaning, a serious meaning. As a matter of fact, these letters stand for two significant but related purposes that highlight why over 1,000 summer and year-round SpringHill leaders run the sprint we call summer camp. It's why they work uncountable hours, at times in uncomfortable weather and conditions, and often endure heartache and disappointment. It's why they experience the joy of loving, serving, teaching, coaching, and leading nearly 28,000 children and students. FTK moves these leaders to do all they can to assure campers have the best week of their year and the most transformative experience of their life.

FTK is also why thousands of supporters, ambassadors, prayer partners, volunteers, churches, and families invest in the work SpringHill does every summer.

It's what drives the SpringHill family, every day, to be more creative in their work, and more effective in serving more kids, families, and churches in more places.

FTK is how we ultimately evaluate the work we do in the summer. It is SpringHill's plumb line. It's what moves us, inspires us, sustains us, and brought all of us together this summer.

And it's why, for the past twenty summers, I've devoted my vocational life serving SpringHill's mission.

The words behind FTK are significant, yet quite straightforward. And as soon as you read them, you'll understand why they are the guiding force of our work.

FTK means For the Kids and For the Kingdom. Hands down, with no serious rivals, there's no better cause, no more important work, no better way to spend a summer than serving His kids and His Kingdom. Just ask the thousands of people who did so this summer and the tens of thousands of kids, families, and churches that experienced the fruit of their work.

For the Kids. For the Kingdom.

ABOUT THE AUTHOR

Michael Perry has been married to Denise since 1984. They have four adult children and one daughter in-law with whom they love to spend time. He's worked for SpringHill since 1998, becoming its President and CEO in 2001.

Before coming to SpringHill, he spent ten years in Human Resources and Quality and Customer Service management at a large, privately held corporation followed by four years as a partner in a number of related startup businesses.

During these years in the "for profit" world, Michael and his wife Denise invested their avocational time in the lives of high school students through the ministry of Young Life where they were volunteer leaders and local committee members. The Perrys spent many of their vacations on long bus rides to exotic places taking hundreds of students to summer camp.

It's been through all these experiences that Michael has discovered his personal mission: to influence Kingdom-building communities and organizations by investing in their current and future leaders.

Michael is a graduate of Central Michigan University with a degree in Business Administration and from Grand Rapids Theological Seminary through Cornerstone University, and he holds an MA in Ministry Leadership, as well. He enjoys fishing, reading, writing, and exploring the world by walking through it.

ABOUT SPRINGHILL

SpringHill is a youth ministry and discipleship organization that uses summer camp experiences to reach young people across the country. From overnight and day camp, to youth retreats and our leadership development experiences, we hope that you will explore ways to get connected to the SpringHill organization.

To learn more about SpringHill, visit springhillcamps.com or on Facebook, Instagram and Twitter at SpringHill Camps.